P9-DBI-073

CANOEING

OUTDOOR PURSUITS SERIES

Laurie Gullion, MS
Outdoor Leadership Program
Greenfield Community College

797.122
GUL

Human Kinetics Publishers

Library of Congress Cataloging-in-Publication Data

Gullion, Laurie.
Canoeing / Laurie Gullion.
p. cm. -- (Outdoor pursuits series)
Includes index.
ISBN 0-87322-443-4
1. Canoes and canoeing. 2. Canoes and canoeing--Equipment and supplies--Evaluation. I. Title. II. Series.
GV783.G85 1994
797.1'22--dc20 93-5599
CIP

ISBN: 0-87322-443-4

Copyright © 1994 by Human Kinetics Publishers

All rights reserved. Except for use in a review, the reproduction or utilization of this work in any form or by any electronic, mechanical, or other means, now known or hereafter invented, including xerography, photocopying, and recording, and in any information storage and retrieval system, is forbidden without the written permission of the publisher.

Acquisitions Editor: Brian Holding; **Series Editor and Developmental Editor:** Holly Gilly; **Assistant Editors:** Valerie Hall, Lisa Sotirelis, and John Wentworth; **Copyeditor:** Molly Bentsen; **Proofreader:** Dawn Roselund; **Indexer:** Theresa J. Schaefer; **Production Director:** Ernie Noa; **Typesetter:** Sandra Meier; **Text Design:** Keith Blomberg; **Text Layout:** Denise Lowry and Tara Welsch; **Cover Photo:** Alan Fortune; **Cover Design:** Jack Davis; **Interior Art:** Thomas • Bradley Illustration & Design; **Interior Photos:** Alan Fortune (additional credits are listed on p. 146); **Author Photo:** Kristin Peterson; **Printer:** Bang Printing

Human Kinetics books are available at special discounts for bulk purchase. Special editions or book excerpts can also be created to specification. For details, contact the Special Sales Manager at Human Kinetics.

Printed in the United States of America 10 9 8 7 6 5 4 3 2 1

Human Kinetics Publishers
Box 5076, Champaign, IL 61825-5076
1-800-747-4457

Canada: Human Kinetics Publishers, Box 24040, Windsor, ON N8Y 4Y9
1-800-465-7301 (in Canada only)

Europe: Human Kinetics Publishers (Europe) Ltd., P.O. Box IW14,
Leeds LS16 6TR, England
0532-781708

Australia: Human Kinetics Publishers, P.O. Box 80, Kingswood 5062, South Australia
618-374-0433

New Zealand: Human Kinetics Publishers, P.O. Box 105-231, Auckland 1
(09) 309-2259

CONTENTS

1

GOING CANOEING

A raised hand from a canoeist in the lead boat signaled the other eight canoes to glide silently to a stop. The paddler pointed to a low hill on the river's north bank, where a muscular, gray-haired wolf was visible in the treeless tundra. Moving along the hillside, the wolf tracked a small band of caribou, creeping closer to a straggler as we watched. Two more wolves crested the hill and joined the pursuit.

Meanwhile, our canoeing group had drifted slowly downriver in the sluggish current, far enough now to be upwind of the animals. Suddenly the wolves caught our scent, abandoned their tracking, and shifted their attention to our silent flotilla. The last caribou disappeared over a nearby hill. We glided out of sight around the bend, talking quietly about the sighting. Fifteen minutes later, a paddler in the back of our pack looked behind him. A lone wolf trotted along the shore, tracking *us* as we continued down the Baillie River in the Barren Lands of sub-Arctic Canada.

That memory is one of my finest of a lifetime of canoeing. Since paddling with my family as a young child, I have enjoyed canoeing's unique vantage point for observing wildlife who seek the water's edge—the diving antics of the common loon, the crash of a moose breaking through shrubs and saplings, the spartan existence of the caribou, grizzly bear, and musk ox in the far north. But most thrilling have been sightings of the wolf—who, contrary to myth, is wary of humans, easily spooked, and often elusive to watch. We met those three wolves again that breezy Arctic day, when they joined their pack on a distant hillside, sat on their haunches like sentinels on watch, and howled a chorus in the dry, crisp air. It was time for us visitors to move along and leave the wolves to their land.

I've canoed more than 6,000 miles in the Northwest Territories of Canada and logged many miles as a whitewater paddler in the continental United States. My favorite trips are those with other canoeists who appreciate the aesthetics of the river environment as much as the inherent thrills of whitewater play, canoeists who appreciate the landscape and the geology that create the watery features within the riverbed. Understanding the life-supporting role of water in the landscape makes paddling my favorite way to explore unusual places, whether urban or wild. Arriving in a city by water is an especially powerful experience, because one realizes the importance of the waterway in our lives and the lack of respect with which we often treat it.

Canoeing the Hood River in the Northwest Territories.

The canoeing experience can provide unlimited satisfaction: exploration of new places, peaceful relaxation, lifetime recreation and fitness, wildlife watching, a renewed understanding of the cultural and economic importance of our waterways. You can gain a wonderful sense of accomplishment from point-to-point paddling or simply handling a solo canoe well on a windy day. You can awaken dormant muscles with a leisurely cruise or enjoy a highly aerobic workout in a local marathon.

Whatever your purpose in beginning to canoe, be open to where the activity can lead you. Do you travel to exotic resorts on vacation? Incorporate a short canoe trip into your plans. Have you moved to a new location or lost touch with friends? Join a regional paddling club to meet new people who share your interests. Do you remember the fun of messing around in canoes at summer camp? Take a canoeing lesson, and discover how to paddle efficiently and elegantly.

The popularity of paddle sports has exploded in the last decade, with an estimated 19 million people now involved in this form of self-propelled travel. Canoeing has a healthy future as more people become oriented to outdoor recreation and seek low-impact ways to explore the environment. Amazing technological advances in durable and light materials have revolutionized boat and equipment design and made canoeing easier than ever for beginners. Gone are the days of heavy, cumbersome boats; enter the era of light, responsive craft that can be lifted by one person. Certainly this development has made canoeing more accessible to people of all ages and abilities.

This book is designed to help you get acquainted with the joys of canoeing and canoe touring. You will learn to make basic decisions easily when purchasing equipment, obtaining professional instruction, and organizing trips. You will gain an understanding of basic paddling principles, which are necessary to paddle efficiently and enjoyably. Knowing common safety guidelines for canoeing will make you a responsible paddler.

You can easily learn canoeing basics in 8 hours, including choosing the right equipment, entering and exiting a boat properly, tracking in a straight line, and rescuing a swamped canoe. I will provide you all the necessary information to organize and complete a safe and enjoyable day tour.

Perhaps the most important ingredient for your development is paddling experience. Your "straight-line" paddling at the outset will probably be more akin to a squiggle! Developing the reflexes and judgment to execute corrective strokes just *before* the boat veers off course usually takes longer than a day. This sensitivity to the water, your paddle, and their effects on your boat simply requires more experience. It may take you 20 to 50 miles (32 to 80 km) of paddling before you feel able to steer instinctively.

With the book's many suggestions for paddling trips, you'll be able to get practice that you need. You'll discover the wealth of opportunities worldwide for embarking on canoeing journeys to new and wonderful places. Refining your skills will happen naturally as you discover new lakes and rivers amid different locales. And because finding other interested canoeists is a common request among beginners, I'll share how to contact paddling clubs and organizations around the world. I'll also offer advice for those interested in expanding their knowledge to become advanced paddlers.

TRANSPORTATION, EXPLORATION, AND RECREATION

When European explorers arrived in the New World in the 1600s, they discovered the canoe to be the primary mode of transportation for native peoples to maintain their hunting and gathering lifestyles. The original canoe—a dugout, or hollowed log boat—had given way to the bark canoe developed by woodland Indians and animal-skin boats developed by the northern Inuit (Eskimo). These lighter, more versatile craft enabled natives and newcomers to easily use the interconnected waterways of North America's interior.

The rivers tied together a vast land, and the versatile, indigenous canoe—which came to be known as the "Canadian canoe" and most resembles today's open canoe—enabled explorers to navigate immense lakes and shallow rivers and to portage over land divides to reach new river basins. As early as the 1700s, traders, or voyageurs, penetrated the Canadian wilderness to send tons of furs from the western Rockies back to the St. Lawrence River for shipment to Europe.

The earliest recreational canoeing was probably native races, but development as a sport became more formal in the 1850s in the Peterborough region of Ontario, where the first plank canoes were built. In the next decade, English barrister John MacGregor returned to Europe with a hybrid design of an oak canoe with sail, propelled by a double-bladed paddle. MacGregor paddled a thousand miles of European rivers in his "Rob Roy," and his popular exploits fueled an explosion of canoe travel for pleasure on both continents.

The public's rising interest in recreation (the bicycling boom occurred simultaneously) launched the canoe as a popular vehicle for activities as diverse as camping and courting. Today, canoeing continues to fascinate us as a means to "get away." It has always been a vehicle for discovery, and it still allows us to explore new places—in the landscape and within ourselves.

Types of Canoeing

The two basic types of canoeing are *solo* (one person) and *tandem* (two people). A solo paddler sits near the middle of the canoe to better control both ends of the craft. Solo canoeing allows you to be independent and to paddle without having to find a partner, which is appealing to many with busy lifestyles. Although every solo paddler experiences some initial frustration, the experience of ultimately controlling your own boat is extremely rewarding.

When paddling solo, sit near the middle of the canoe for better control.

Tandem canoeing lets you work cooperatively, which has its own rewards and frustrations. Many people prefer the sociability of tandem canoeing and like the additional power created by two people. The challenges are developing an effective communication system and sharing responsibilities. The bow paddler (in the front of the canoe) sets the tempo while the stern paddler (in the back) keeps the boat on track while matching the bow person's pace.

With the strokes you will learn in *Canoeing*, you will be able to paddle both tandem and solo crafts. The same basic strokes have different effects on the boat because you sit in different places; these effects will become second nature as you spend time on the water.

When paddling tandem, good communication is necessary.

Learning basic maneuvers will let you enjoy a variety of general recreational paddling activities, from fishing to bird-watching to longer day tours. If you like point-to-point travel, you may want to combine your canoeing skills with camping. Canoe camping provides an enjoyable way to experience outdoor overnights without having to carry a backpack. (The canoe carries the weight of your gear; you only need to heft it up on shore!) For families with young children, canoe camping can be a perfect introduction to the outdoors.

The skills taught in this book lay a good foundation for exploring other types of canoeing. Easy whitewater runs might be your next step if you like the idea of negotiating wilder currents among obstacles in the river.

Perhaps you'll want to explore canoe racing. Many local races feature recreational classes for newcomers; you get exposure to experienced racers and an opportunity to watch their technique as well as a great workout. I'll teach you the dynamics of a strong forward stroke that can make you an effective recreational racer.

Not really interested in racing? Consider freestyle paddling. These paddlers like to play on flatwater and create a series of acrobatic moves. The canoes can be leaned for dramatic effect while turning, and the

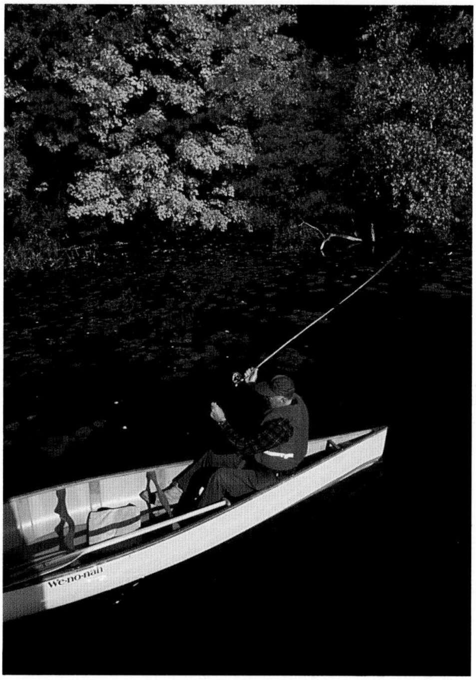

Fishing is just one of many recreational activities you can enjoy in a canoe.

challenge is to remain upright when trying more difficult moves. Freestyle paddlers also stage competitions, which remind me of ice-skating venues. Choreographed moves are set to music, and judges award points for the difficulty and aesthetic appeal of the presentation. The moves you'll practice with the help of this book are used commonly by freestyle paddlers.

Basic principles, strokes, and maneuvers are the common thread between all paddle sports, and they provide you with the foundation to become a solid multidiscipline paddler and explore other paddle sports like whitewater canoeing and kayaking. Although the focus in this book is general recreational canoeing and touring, with further instruction and experience you can modify the basic techniques to suit the demands of a particular paddle sport.

What Type of Canoeing Interests You?

Deciding which type of canoeing to explore depends on your personality, the nature of the water in your region, the type of paddler you want to be, and, in tandem paddling, your partner's desires. (Making this decision a joint one increases the chance of success for a paddling partnership.)

As an instructor, I find it disturbing to see people be coerced into paddling activities in which they have no interest or comfort. I've also fielded many questions from students about their concerns in learning to canoe. Use the following questions to help you determine the kind of canoeing that's right for you.

FIND YOUR CANOEING NICHE

Assess your personal needs, and be honest with any potential partners about your preferences. Your paddling comfort and long-term enjoyment of canoeing are at stake here. Consider these important questions in analyzing your preferences:

1. Are you worried about physical strength, especially of your upper body? Consider beginning with tandem rather than solo canoeing. Plan short-term sessions until you can assess your physical abilities. Remember that efficient strokes can compensate for physical strength.
2. Are you nervous on the water, perhaps due to limited swimming skills? Canoe stability may be important to you. A sheltered location can also ease your introduction. You may actually be more comfortable paddling a canoe solo, where you know who is controlling (tipping!) the boat. However, others might feel more secure in tandem canoeing.
3. Do you like to visit new places? Plan short tours at first. Especially if you include kids, choose a route with interesting points along the way and at your final destination to keep interest high and fidgeting low.
4. Is aerobic conditioning a priority? Find a partner who shares that enthusiasm and wants to cruise at the same pace. Or paddle solo in a canoe designed for straight-ahead speed.
5. Do you eventually want excitement and challenge in your canoeing? You may want to explore whitewater canoeing once you've gotten some experience. Develop equally your abilities to spin the boat quickly and to paddle straight on flatwater, which are necessary before you attempt whitewater canoeing.

If you have a limited history of participation in other recreational activities, then plan a shorter introduction to canoeing—perhaps several hours or a half day with plenty of options for stopping sooner if you need to. One of the nicest benefits of canoeing is that it can be slow-paced, which is why it appeals to people with limited exposure to the outdoors. Even though I do a lot of backpacking, mostly on cross-country skis, I

If you're just beginning canoeing, take it slow. You might be surprised at the simple pleasure of moving on water.

still prefer canoeing because I'd rather let the canoe carry the weight of my gear during the day.

The virtue of canoeing is that it offers enjoyment to people of all ages and abilities with very different needs. Whether your aim is to keep adding new rivers and lakes to your paddling list or to go bird-watching on the local pond, canoeing can accommodate your desires.

Narrowing your preference is helpful when you prepare to purchase equipment. With almost a thousand different canoes on the market, the choices become less bewildering as you focus your interest. If you're unsure, know that a general recreational canoe is a great way to begin and is typically easy to sell if later you decide on a more specialized boat.

Getting Started

Before you invest time and money in equipment, you need to experience canoeing! Many exciting and inexpensive opportunities await you. Your introduction will be most successful if you seek the wisdom of experienced canoeists. Canoeing alone is *not* recommended for beginners. Take advantage of any local opportunities to begin your canoeing education.

SAFETY TIP Begin wisely. Learn with a support group. Do not paddle alone.

"Demo Days" and Expositions

Canoeing manufacturers and outfitters often offer free opportunities for the public to mess around in their boats. Many newcomers find this exposure invaluable. The manufacturers of course hope you'll invest in equipment, but the short-term exposure gets you involved and expands your knowledge. Some instruction may be available, but most often you are simply allowed to try out many different kinds of boats in the practice area. Special talks by knowledgeable canoeists may also be scheduled, and you can gain valuable insights from these experts.

Instructional Centers

A reputable center will not only teach you how to canoe, but its instructors will provide you with helpful information on small but important points: how to carry and load a canoe, how to pack a boat and keep it "trim," how to warm up and stretch for paddling, how to rescue a swamped canoe, and how to practice safely. An important feature of competent, professional instruction is providing you with enough personal feedback that you leave the lesson with a clear prescription for practice. Various canoeing and outdoors publications feature seasonal lists of instructional centers and schools that specialize in paddling instruction.

CONSUMER TIP Responsible instruction builds safety and rescue skills as well as good canoeing technique.

Paddling Clubs

Local and regional clubs provide an excellent and inexpensive way for you to meet other canoeing enthusiasts and get introductory instruction. Most clubs list outings for a variety of ability levels—from short to long tours in locations that range from urban to remote. You need not own a canoe to participate. If the club doesn't own a fleet of canoes (many do), enthusiastic members are likely to loan you gear to get started. When you're ready to purchase equipment, you'll also find a crew of personal shoppers ready to accompany you. (Canoeists are often passionate about their activity!) Most importantly, club trips provide a support group ready to aid in rescue efforts if boats tip over. This safety network is sacrificed when you paddle alone.

Travel Tours

Travel tours, from spartan to plush, make canoeing a vacation experience. Popular inn-to-inn tours give you a taste of the activity, cushioned by hot showers and gourmet meals at the end of the day. They are a great way to begin, particularly for families. Responsible tour organizations offer instruction at the beginning of the program, establish clear group organization on the water, and monitor your progress throughout the day. Adventure tours take you into more remote locations, usually for longer periods, and offer even greater emphasis on instruction and preparedness. These companies are also listed in the directories of outdoors and canoeing magazines.

On Your Way!

Any of these options will get you started. The demo days are less likely to offer any concrete instruction, so it's wise to follow up that exposure with an instructional experience of some kind. I don't recommend you begin by renting equipment from a local outfitter unless the rental includes a minilesson on strokes and water safety. I've had many a self-taught paddler seek help in a lesson after becoming frustrated with a continuing inability to keep a canoe going straight.

Simple paddling about can seem so easy that instruction would be unnecessary. But boats do like to turn (some more quickly than others), and with instructional tips you'll more quickly learn the easy tricks that keep your canoe on course. Instruction also teaches you to paddle well, which to me means paddling efficiently. I like to get a good return for energy expended, and efficient paddling lets me paddle stronger and farther (and look great in the process).

Once you've decided how you want to begin your canoeing experience, you'll need to get equipped. Chapter 2 helps you select the right clothing for paddling in different seasons and choose the right gear for your size and the type of canoeing.

THE FREEDOM OF CANOEING

Hip surgery had left octogenarian Lois Harris with limited mobility on uneven terrain. She thought a weekend canoeing trip on a rural section of the Connecticut River in western Massachusetts was a lovely idea—for other people. An avid canoeist since her Girl Scouting days early in this century, she reminisced to her friend Marion Stoddart about the pleasure canoeing had given her.

Stoddart had just begun an outdoors business for women 40 years and older, and she called me to see whether the Connecticut River trip, with 15 miles of paddling and riverside tent camping, might be suitable for Lois. Canoeing offers great mobility and freedom to a person who cannot walk easily or at all, so it was no problem unless sitting in a boat caused discomfort. The primary issue was Lois's mobility on land, and there she would have plenty of helping hands.

A contributor to the sections on aging in the latest edition of *Our Bodies, Our Selves* (a comprehensive book on women's issues), Lois was persuaded to join our trip. Her enthusiasm inspired the rest of the group, and her paddling abilities elicited admiration, if not a little envious frustration! This diminutive woman had forgotten little of her Girl Scout training, and Lois stroked her way energetically down the river, talking to her partner nonstop. The fact that most of the other canoeists spent the trip looking at Lois's backside caused a fair amount of discussion and good-natured ribbing—when they could catch up!

A raw rain fell on the second day, and Lois ate lunch cheerfully, water streaming off her hat. She remarked that one just can't let "things"—whether a bad hip, a poor attitude, or miserable weather—get in the way of trying new endeavors, and she was so glad that she had decided to come. That Lois took a chance impressed her companions, most of whom were canoeing novices, and they left the trip motivated to continue their paddling and their explorations of the outdoors.

2

CANOEING EQUIPMENT

I began acquiring paddling gear the easy way. When I quit my job as a newspaper reporter to begin teaching outdoor activities, at a farewell party my co-workers gave me a paddle and a lifejacket—as well as a lot of good-natured support for what I'm sure they perceived as a dubious change of career. Then my parents gave a canoe to my husband and me as a wedding present (which started a trend in gift-giving among marrying friends for the next few years). But don't think that quitting your job or getting married is a prerequisite to building your own equipment locker!

But it worked for me—so well that our supply of boats has outgrown a two-car garage and forced us to build extra storage. We operate under a principle common to many paddlers that having limited gear might interfere with our desire to outfit fleets of visiting friends and relatives. Better to be prepared with plenty of gear in lots of shapes and sizes. We've acquired most of our equipment by bartering with other paddlers and watching announcement boards in local shops and instructional schools for notices of used gear. Be forewarned—this consuming and enjoyable pastime is likely to accompany your growing love of canoeing.

If relatives and friends don't act on your hints that paddling gear makes great presents, then it's time to begin your own shopping. Choosing the right equipment from an array of new products is the challenge. If you buy poorly fitting equipment or items that are not designed for your purposes, your enjoyment of canoeing may suffer. But if you find yourself in this predicament, remember that it's usually quite easy to sell used gear.

Select equipment that is likely to match your needs most of the time. Most people adopt a general approach at first, before they are sure of their paddling preferences. They can take advantage of the very good general recreational gear on the market today. However, if a specialized activity interests you more strongly, then head in that more specific direction right from the beginning. For instance, if canoe touring is your major interest, you'll appreciate the special features of a touring boat. The longer, narrower boat goes straighter than a general recreational model. You can always borrow or rent a canoe for those occasions when you might want a different style.

The best way to learn about canoeing equipment is to test it out. Although information from knowledgeable salespeople and canoeists is helpful, there is no substitute for actually using the equipment and comparing different designs. You'll know a sluggish or tipsy boat when you paddle it! You *can* feel how it responds in the water. Just carrying the boat to the water will tell you whether the canoe is a manageable weight for you.

You'll find it easier and less expensive to acquire other paddling accessories first. Basic equipment includes clothing appropriate to the season, a paddle, and a personal flotation device (PFD).

Try canoeing out before you purchase a paddle and PFD. Once you decide you want to canoe more often, then invest in personal gear. I know many paddlers who canoe only five or six times a year, but they own their own PFDs and paddles. Equipment that is sized exactly to their body enhances their enjoyment.

What Gear Is Available?

The market for gear is greater than ever as manufacturers continue to develop new designs for a public increasingly eager to try canoeing. More than 900 different types of canoes are available at a wide variety of prices. Whether your need is specialized design or all-purpose equipment at an affordable price, there is something for you.

Advanced technologies have helped spawn the many new designs at a range of prices in boats, paddles, and accessories. Unless you love techno-speak, you needn't clutter your head with subtle technical nuances. A certain amount of terminology is helpful, but don't be afraid to cut through the jargon and ask your advisor to speak in simple, functional terms.

Beyond design, manufacturers have also developed new product lines to meet the needs of a variety of canoeists, particularly families. The increase in products tailored to children is a heartening development. I've seen children slip out of adult-sized PFDs or poorly designed kids' models, but new products have special features that enhance their safety.

Choosing the Proper Clothing and Accessories

The inevitability of getting wet, even if it's just from paddle splash, is an important consideration when you dress to canoe. The possibility of capsizing always exists, and it often happens when you least expect it. I've seen many people trip getting out of their canoes near shore, soaking themselves in a mere foot of water.

Dressing for Success

The best clothing for canoeing is loose, quick-drying apparel that feels comfortable when you're sitting and doesn't restrict your torso movement. Choose roomy shorts and pants that don't bind when you sit. Synthetic materials that dry quickly will keep you warmer and more comfortable in the canoe. Outside of the summer months, avoid cotton garments, which remain wet and cold with no insulating ability. I always wear a nylon bathing suit under my layers, even in cooler weather, because wet cotton underwear leaves an uncomfortable clammy feeling.

Be prepared for cooler temperatures, especially from wind on large bodies of water, and remember that water temperature, rather than air temperature, is the more important consideration. Even on summer days, river and lake temperatures can drop to 50 to 60 degrees F (10 to 15 degrees C), which can cool you rapidly after a capsize. It's wise to always be prepared for an unexpected swim.

The following items of clothing are advisable, especially for cool-weather/cool-water paddling. Prices are in U.S. dollars.

Anorak ($50-$250). A waterproof or windproof anorak (a hooded jacket that zips from neck to midchest) can vie for the honor of most-used item of clothing. Canoeists can handle many quickly changing conditions with this item. I find the models with large front pockets very handy for keeping lip salve, sunscreen, bug repellent, and the like easily accessible. Aim for function over fashion!

Paddling jacket ($75-$200). As an alternative to an anorak, some prefer to wear a paddling jacket, usually made of coated nylon with neck and wrist cuffs to prevent water infiltration.

Select equipment that is likely to match your needs most of the time; the best way to learn about equipment is to test it out!

Pullover ($50-$150). A synthetic sweater or pullover provides extra insulation and sheds water when wet. Wool stays wet but still provides warmth. Some pullovers are made specifically to wear under paddling jackets, with a lowcut neck and shorter sleeves.

Rain gear ($75-$250). A two-piece coated-nylon or Goretex rainsuit is best. Avoid ponchos and cagoules (long raincoats), because they are cumbersome if you capsize. Cagoules also make it difficult to get in and out of the canoe. Bodies of water have a way of creating and attracting storm systems, so don't leave home without rain protection.

Undergarments ($15-$40). Synthetic or wool long underwear will keep you warm if you get wet. I like wearing nylon shorts over long underwear on cool days; the combination dries faster than twill pants.

Footwear ($20-$80). Foot protection from shore litter, like broken glass, is essential, and a sturdy-soled shoe or sandal will prevent injury. Don't skimp here; get a thick-soled shoe. Footwear also needs to be form-fitting so that it doesn't fall off during a capsize. River sandals, rubber-soled "water socks," and neoprene booties are designed specifically for paddling. Buy the thick-soled models for better protection.

Headgear ($5-$25). Almost 75% of your body heat escapes through the head and neck. A wool hat is essential to staying warm. A baseball or similar hat with a brim provides protection against the sun. Sunglasses also minimize the glare reflected off water.

SAFETY TIP Dress for the water temperature, not the air temperature.

Handy Accessories

Personal preparedness goes beyond clothing and includes accessories and first aid readiness. I've seen more accidents on shore than on water, when people load and unload boats or carry them to and from the water. Splinters and cut feet are more common than exotic capsizing scenes. Don't let a lack of first aid supplies jeopardize your canoeing.

Tailor the amount of first aid gear to the size and needs of your group. Know the medical history of every group member, and check on everyone's current health before you leave on a a tour, whether a day trip or longer. For instance, a person with a known allergy to bee stings would want to include an antivenom kit, because a quick exit off a lake or river can be difficult.

Dry Bag or Box ($10-$120). This waterproof container protects extra clothing, food, first aid, and cameras. Dry boxes come in a variety of sizes if you want to compartmentalize your gear. Large plastic containers with handles are great; check a bakery for frosting containers, a fish store for herring buckets, a carpenter for joint compound containers!

First Aid Kit ($25-$100). General commercial kits are available, but the best approach is to develop a kit that matches your first aid skills and the remoteness of your canoeing.

Choosing the Right PFD

Don't assume that being a good swimmer makes a personal flotation device (PFD) unnecessary. Even the best swimmers benefit from the security of PFDs in cold water, swift water, cold weather, or canoe rescues, which can be chaotic.

BASIC FIRST AID CHECKLIST

- Triangular bandage
- Gauze roll and pads
- Band-Aids
- Moleskin
- Adhesive tape
- Aspirin
- Acetaminophen
- Personal medications
- Elastic bandage
- Antiseptic cleaning solution
- Coins for emergency phone calls
- Paper and pencil (for rescue information)
- Local emergency phone numbers
- Tweezers
- Scissors
- Chemical water treatment tablets
- Sunscreen
- Bug repellent
- Reusable ice pack

Don't Leave Shore Without It

Wearing a PFD is strongly recommended for flatwater canoeing and essential for whitewater rivers. All states require that you have personal flotation of some kind in the canoe, but some now mandate the actual wearing of life vests in certain seasons. Check the regulations in your locale, but remember that it just makes good sense to be prepared for a capsize by wearing a vest-style PFD at all times.

A U.S. Coast Guard–approved Type III PFD ($40-$90) is the vest model usually used by canoeists, because its construction provides adequate flotation in rough, inland waters. A Type III PFD also protects your torso from abrasion and provides extra warmth on cold days.

A Type III PFD keeps your head above water in the event of a capsize, although you have to tip your head backward to avoid a face-down position. Some models with extra flotation are designed to keep the head of an unconscious person tipped backward. Children's models ($40-$50) have flotation collars that provide the same function and leg straps to prevent the wearer from slipping out of the PFD. Most children's models come in two sizes: small (19- to 23-inch, or 48- to 58-cm, chest) and medium (24- to 29-inch, or 59- to 74-cm, chest).

The flotation foam in a PFD is sewn into a nylon cover as broad, flat panels or as tubes that run vertically in narrow pockets. New form-fitting jackets provide more freedom of movement with large armholes, but they offer less flotation and they may not be USCG-approved.

Avoid ''horse collar'' kapok (Type II) models that drape uncomfortably around your neck. Throwable flotation devices like Type IV boat cushions are handy as backup rescue devices, but they shouldn't be substituted for a Type III life vest. It's hard to rescue a canoe or to swim while using a cushion.

PFDs are essential for any canoeing outing.

AT A GLANCE: PFDs

Flotation	*Strengths*	*Weaknesses*	*Price*
Foam panels	Less bulk Good protection	More expensive	\$50-\$80
Foam tubes	Least expensive Good protection	More bulk	\$40-\$70
Form-fitting	Least bulk Freedom of movement	Most expensive Less flotation	\$50-\$90

Wearing a PFD Properly

A properly fitting PFD will fit snugly around your torso without inhibiting your mobility, and it will stay in place when you float in the water. If the PFD slides up and obscures your vision, it is too big. Test the fit in a store by asking a friend to pull up on the vest. If it rides up near your chin or obscures your vision, it's either too big or not cinched properly. Also make sure your PFD fits comfortably over layers of clothing: if it doesn't, you are less likely to wear it. Follow these tips for best results when you wear your PFD:

- Zip the PFD up completely.
- Tie or buckle the waistband tightly.
- Cinch in any adjustment straps on the sides and front.

Choosing a Paddle

Treat yourself to a well-balanced paddle! You don't have to be a design engineer to recognize a heavy, awkward paddle when it's in your hands. After learning to canoe at summer camp with paddling “clubs,” I'm convinced that the lighter the paddle, the better the introduction.

Before you select a paddle, you should know the basic parts, including the grip (handle), shaft, blade, throat (where the blade attaches to the shaft), and tip.

FIND THE PADDLE THAT'S RIGHT FOR YOU

1. A blade that's longer (25 inches, or 63.5 cm) and narrower (5 to 6 inches, or 13 to 15 cm) gives less resistance against the water while touring. It's also quieter.
2. A wider blade (7 to 8 inches, or 18 to 20 cm) provides more power for racing or whitewater paddling.
3. A stiff paddle is best in whitewater; a more flexible paddle is better for general paddling.
4. Too much flex, particularly in older, plastic paddles, interferes with the ability to transmit power against the blade.
5. A square-tipped blade can catch in the water; beginners may prefer a blade with rounded edges for easier control.

Initially, you'll appreciate a longer, narrower blade with rounded edges at the tip for general recreational canoeing or touring. My favorite choice is a wooden paddle ($20-$175), despite the expense of laminated models, because it feels warmer, lighter, and more responsive. I periodically need to touch up the varnish, but I don't mind the repairs.

The most inexpensive paddles ($15) combine an aluminum shaft with a plastic blade, and these maintenance-free models are fine at the beginning. However, the shaft can get cold, and the plastic blade can get “noodle-y” and provide limited resistance against the water. In some paddles, an

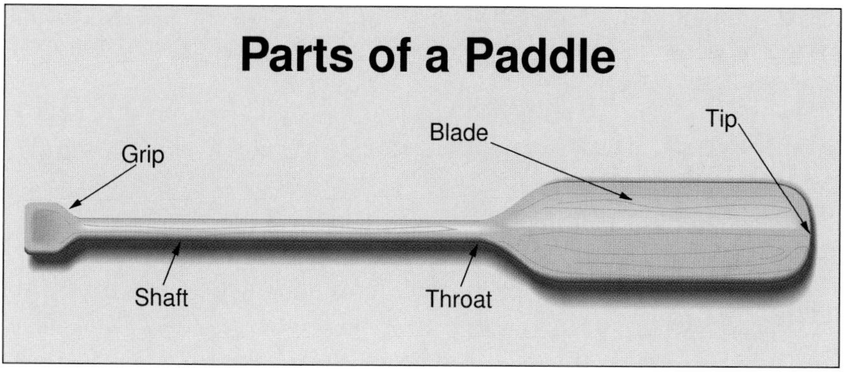

Before you buy a paddle, learn the basic parts.

aluminum shaft is covered with a plastic sheath and the blade is fiberglass ($75). The most expensive paddles use new synthetic materials like foam cores and Kevlar, or graphite for extreme lightness ($150-$250).

Paddle Grips

The two major types of grips are the T and the pear. The T allows a firm grasp and precise control of the blade for turning strokes. Whitewater paddlers definitely prefer them, but many flatwater paddlers also like the control factor. The pear grip provides a better platform for the hands

Types of grips, shafts, and materials are some of the options you can choose from when selecting a paddle.

during straight-ahead power stroking, and most flatwater racing paddles have pear grips. It also allows easy twirling of the paddle during freestyle canoeing moves.

Because I paddle all types of water, I usually purchase paddles with T grips. If you plan to paddle primarily flatwater, a pear grip will work nicely.

Straight or Bent Shaft?

A straight shaft is easier to manipulate for turning strokes and backward paddling. It stores more easily in a canoe when you're camping. The bent shaft creates a bend of 5 to 17 degrees between the blade and shaft. The forward angle of the shaft puts the blade in a perpendicular position at the end of a forward stroke and eliminates any lifting of water at the end of strokes, which slows the canoe.

Flatwater racers use bent-shaft paddles for efficient, powerful stroking. Bow paddlers on a recreational tour also can use bent-shaft paddles, since their primary job is generating speed. A tandem stern paddler who is touring is more likely to use a straight-shaft paddle to more easily execute corrective strokes and keep the boat tracking straight.

A straight-shafted paddle is initially the more versatile choice. Later you may want to purchase a bent shaft for faster cruising or to run recreational races in your area.

Sizing a Canoe Paddle

Run from any helpful person who tells you to measure a paddle from the floor to your chin. Your leg length is not the important measurement. Your torso length, the canoe seat height, and your paddling style determine the proper paddle length. When you're seated in a canoe, your height above the water is a function of your torso length and the canoe seat height (which can vary from 17 to 30 cm). The higher your stance, the longer the paddle needs to be. The two methods illustrated on page 24 work for finding the right paddle length.

Depending on torso size, most tandem canoeists need a paddle between 54 inches (137 cm) and 58 inches (147 cm). Add about 2 inches (5 cm) if you need the extra reach for carving turns in solo, freestyle, or whitewater canoeing. Subtract 2 inches for a bent-shaft paddle to be used in high-powered racing. The shorter paddle will let you stroke a higher tempo.

Test a paddle before you buy it, and trust your instincts. If the paddle drags through the water, the blade may be too big and will provide too

AT A GLANCE: PADDLES

Material	*Strengths*	*Weaknesses*	*Price*
Plastic	Very inexpensive Durable	Heavy Unresponsive	$12-$20
Aluminum and plastic	Very inexpensive Light	Plastic blade flexes with age. Plastic blade can crack. Aluminum shaft feels cold.	$16-$25
Aluminum and fiberglass	Light Good midrange price Aluminum shaft is often wrapped in plastic sheath.	Tip of fiberglass blade can abrade.	$20-$90
Wood	Light Warm feel Flexes slightly. Laminated wood is attractive.	Requires maintenance. Better laminates can be expensive.	$20-$175
Foam/Kevlar/ graphite	Light Responsive	Expensive	$150-$250

much resistance. If your grip hand is above your head during strokes, the paddle is too long. If the paddle feels heavy in the store, imagine how its weight will seem after a few hours of paddling. When in doubt, go light.

Choosing a Canoe

Like any activity, canoeing has its jargon, and some enthusiasts may confound you with technical language in an attempt to be helpful. Learn a few basic terms and ask well-meaning advisors, particularly salespeople, to keep it simple. Refer to the glossary when necessary to clarify the meanings of terms and to improve your knowledge.

Method 1: On the Water

1. Sit comfortably in the canoe on water.
2. Place the paddle perpendicular to the water surface with the blade submerged to the throat. This position duplicates a correct forward stroke.
3. The top of the paddle grip should reach to your nose.

Method 2: Without Water

1. With your feet on the ground, crouch down and elevate your buttocks until they reach the approximate height of the canoe seat you're likely to use.
2. Invert your paddle so the grip rests on the floor and the blade is near your face. On a paddle of correct length, the throat of the blade should reach to your nose.

What the Hull Shape Means

The shape of the hull below the waterline affects the canoe's ability to track straight. Boats may have a *V* shape to improve tracking and allow some sideways maneuvering. The greater the *V*, the sharper the tracking. The canoe has less initial stability when the boat rests flat on the water and more secondary stability when it leans to the side. I like this design in a first canoe because it offers you many options. The boat tracks reasonably well on flatwater, but its maneuverability and good secondary stability also allow you to paddle easy whitewater.

Other canoes have a flatter bottom at the waterline, which can greatly enhance sideways maneuverability. These boats also have good initial stability but can have less secondary stability, particularly when bouncing in waves.

The shape of the hull above the waterline also has an impact. Boats with *tumblehome*—the hull curves inward above the waterline—have less secondary stability in waves. Tumblehome is a nice benefit in a flatwater canoe, because the paddler can more comfortably reach the water. Canoes

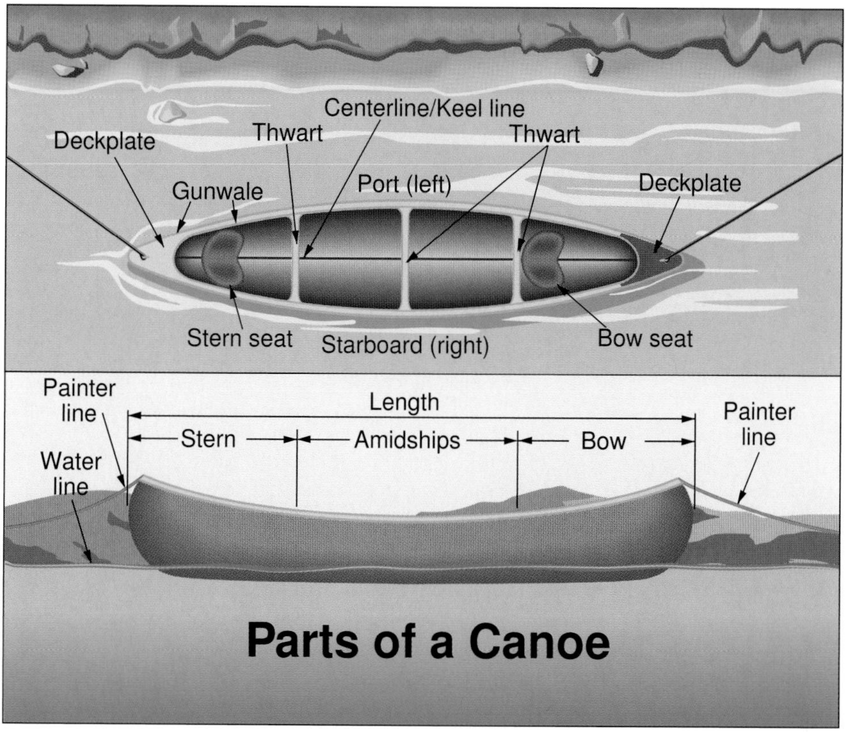

Before purchasing or renting a canoe, you'll want to learn the basic terms.

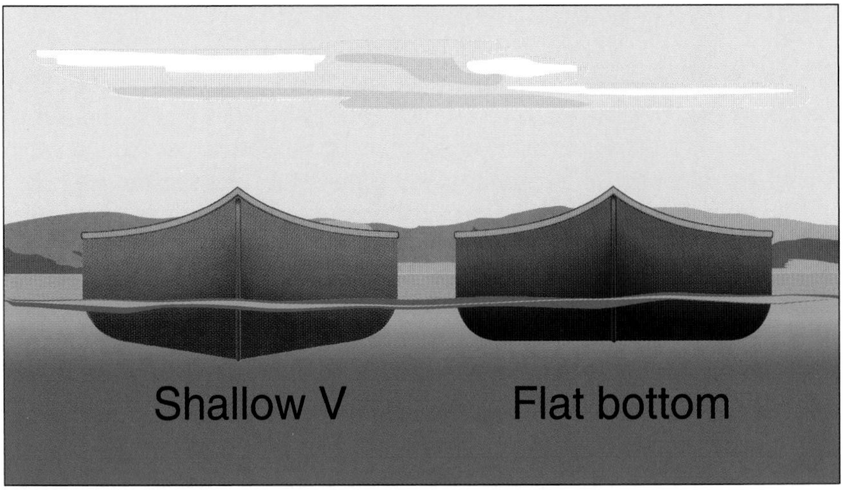

A flat-bottom canoe provides good initial stability, but for better secondary stability, choose a *V*-shaped bottom.

with *flared* hulls have more buoyancy and handle waves better, so they are often found in whitewater craft.

A characteristic with great impact on tracking ability is the shape of the ends of the canoe. The straighter the *stem* (end), the better the canoe will track. The greater the curve, the easier the canoe will turn. The degree

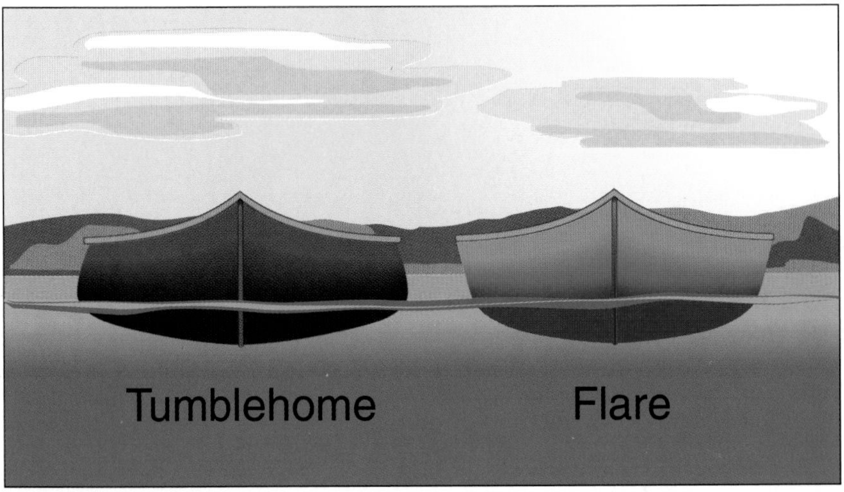

A canoe with tumblehome is good for flatwater; for whitewater, a canoe with a flared hull is a better choice.

to which a boat's hull shape is curved from bow to stern is called *rocker*. A canoe with a lot of rocker will turn very easily.

A keel is a narrow ridge that protrudes from a canoe's underside, running from the bow to the stern straight down the center of the boat. Keels, which make boats track more easily, are usually found in wooden or aluminum boats. A *flatwater* keel is sharper and longer (1 to 1-1/2 inches, or 2-1/2 to 4 cm) than the modified keel (1/2-inch, or 1.3 cm) of a whitewater model. This shorter keel, like the classic ''shoe'' keel of an aluminum whitewater canoe, allows easier sideways maneuverability.

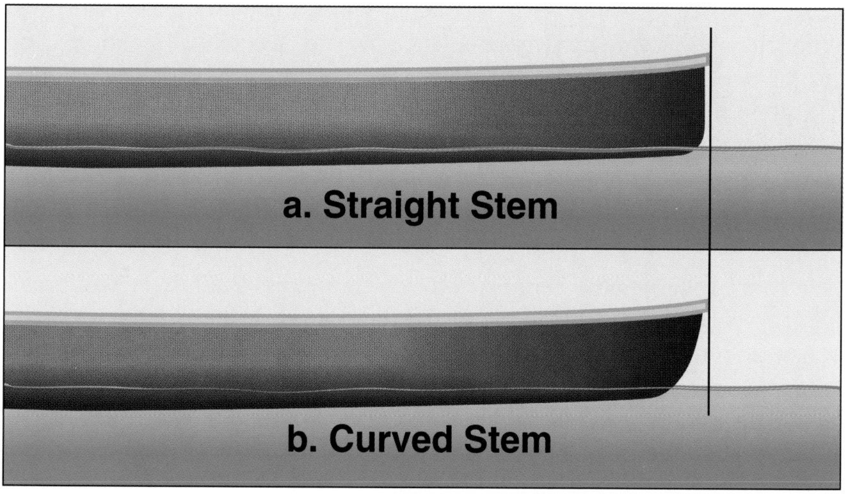

The shape of the end of the canoe helps determine how well the canoe will track and turn.

A Wealth of Materials

The earliest canoes were wooden; next came wood and canvas, then aluminum (after World War II when Grumman applied aircraft technology to boats), fiberglass, and now plastic and Kevlar construction. Boat durability has increased dramatically with new materials that have allowed a wealth of new designs. The materials from which a canoe is made affect four major areas: strength, weight, durability, and cost.

Many people remember aluminum canoes from summer camp, and today's campers are probably still using the boats in which you paddled. I teach in a college outdoor leadership program, where the aluminum canoes were purchased more than 20 years ago. A used aluminum canoe, complete with the inevitable dents, is still a good purchase.

Advanced technology in plastics has created a new series of ABS (acrylonitrile butadiene styrene) and polyethylene boats. ABS boats sandwich a foam core between two thin plastic layers, which creates a laminated surface that slips easily over logs and rocks. Polyethylene boats are created from powdered plastic resins, which are heated in an aluminum mold to 500 degrees F (260 degrees C) in huge ovens. This process creates a durable surface in a less expensive boat.

Fiberglass allows manufacturers to construct a sharper stem for more efficient tracking, and the material repairs easily. It isn't as durable as Kevlar, a material also used in bulletproof vests, which creates lighter and stronger boats. Kevlar, though, is more expensive. Wooden canoes can be equally as or more expensive than Kevlar, according to the craftsmanship involved, but their aesthetic appeal cannot be overlooked. Wooden boats require more maintenance than the new plastic technologies, but many consider their beauty worth it.

Use the canoe materials comparison chart, reprinted by permission of *canoe* magazine, to analyze the differences in materials.

Basic Boat Types

Flatwater canoes can be simplified to four basic types tailored to different types of paddling. Each type is available in tandem and solo models. If you want a multipurpose craft for your first canoe, then a general recreational model is a wise choice. If you want to focus your canoeing interests later with a more specialized boat, the general canoe is easy to resell.

General recreational canoes are designed for a variety of purposes, from fishing to whitewater paddling. They tend to be stable, maneuverable, and durable, but their versatility also makes them lower in performance than more specialized craft. They do not track as well as touring canoes. Construction can range from more inexpensive polyethylene to wood. Low maintenance is often a characteristic, which makes them good starter canoes. They can carry a moderate volume of gear and are suitable for overnight camping.

The longer, narrower boats used for touring track well, which makes them faster than general recreational boats. Often they are not as quickly maneuverable; though they function best on flatwater, they can handle easy current. They are also suitable for carrying camping gear, even the high volume often required by long-distance travel.

Racing canoes are even longer and narrower, streamlined for fast straight-ahead performance at the expense of maneuverability and stability. They are most often used by skilled canoeists for fitness conditioning or racing. A racing canoe has a lower profile, is tippier than cruising craft, and is built to established racing specifications.

Freestyle canoes emphasize secondary stability over initial stability so the boats can be leaned for dramatic effect. Usually shorter than other canoes, they offer a compromise between tracking and maneuverability.

Canoe Materials Comparison Chart

	Cost	Complex shapes	Resist abrasion	Human comfort	Resist impact	Ease over rocks	Repairs	Weight
Polyethylene (unidirectional)	Low	Yes	Fair	Good	Good	Good	Hard	Heavy
Polyethylene (cross-linked)	Mod low	Yes	Fair	Good	Good	Good	Very hard	Heavy
Aluminum	Low–mid	No	Good	Poor	Fair	Poor	Easy	Mod heavy
Fiberglass (chopper gun)	Low	Yes	Poor	Good	Poor	Good	Easy	Very heavy
Fiberglass (cloth)	Middle	Yes	Good	Good	Good	Good	Easy	Mod light
Royalex (ABS)	Hi–med	Yes	Fair	Very good	Very good	Very good	Fairly hard	Mod light
Kevlar	High	Yes	Good	Good	Tear resistance: very good Impact resistance: good	Good	Fairly easy	Light
Composites with nylon, graphite	Very high	Yes	Good	Good	Good	Good	Fairly easy	Very light
Wood	High	Yes	Good	Very good	Good	Good	Easy	Mod light

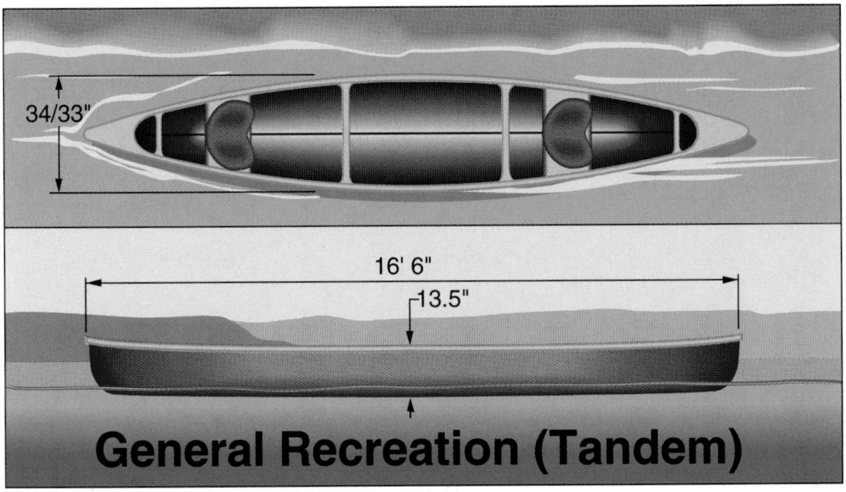

Canoes for general recreation are stable, durable, and versatile, but they lack the high performance of a specialized craft.

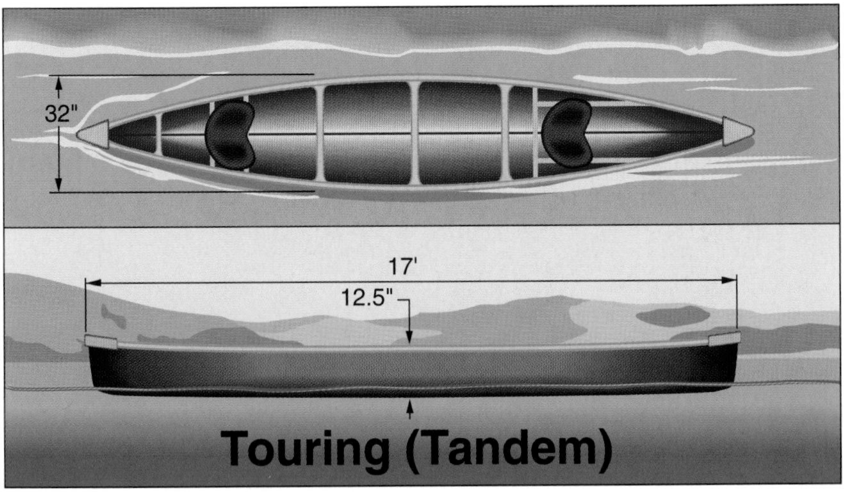

The longer, narrower touring canoes are faster than general recreational canoes.

Renting Gear

It's time to begin comparison shopping. You can test-drive canoeing equipment by renting gear from a local outfitter or instructional school. Remember to ask these organizations or retailers about any used equipment for sale.

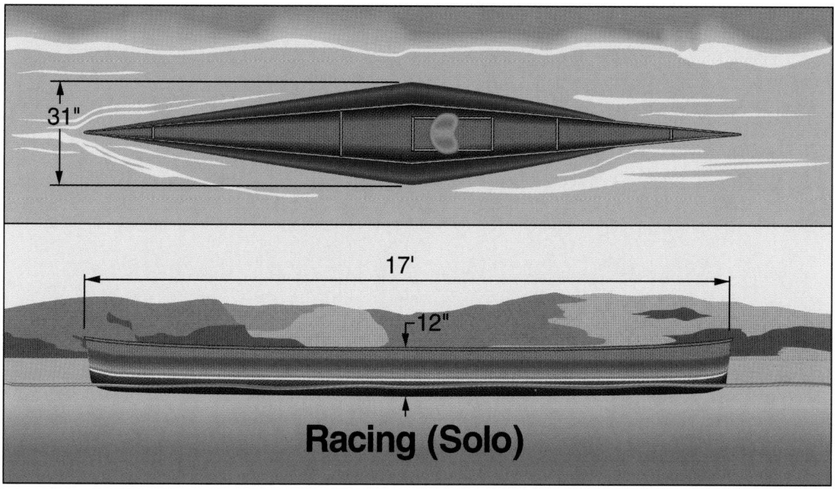

Racing canoes are fast at the expense of stability and maneuverability.

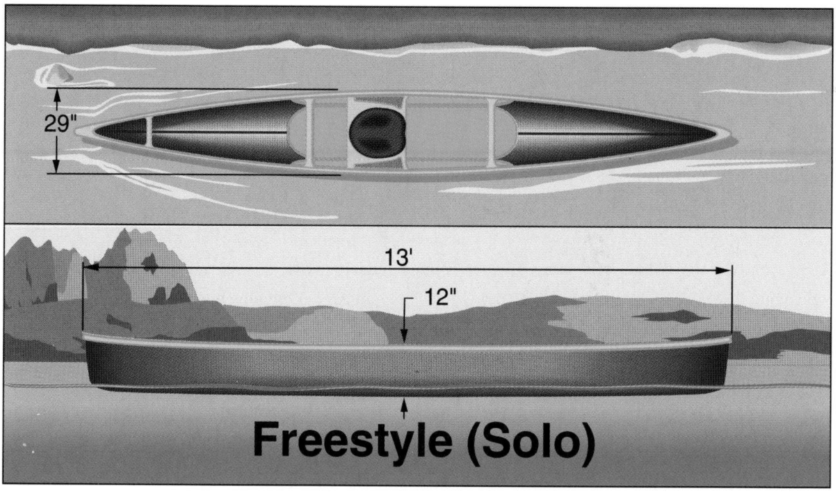

A freestyle canoe might be the best choice for canoeists who are near small ponds and lakes.

Reputable outfitters and dealers check their rental and used equipment carefully, but other outfitters don't. You should ask yourself these questions when conducting your own safety inspection.

- Does the canoe have any damaged thwarts, gunwales, seats, or deckplates?
- Is the hull in good repair or is it patched?

- Do you see dents in the keel or bow when you sight along its line?
- Are the painter lines tied solidly to the canoe?
- Do paddles have cracked blades or loose grips?
- Does the PFD have a working zipper and are adjustment straps in good condition?
- Are any foam panels or tubes exposed by rips in the PFD's nylon covering?

Ask to exchange equipment in poor repair. Your inspection is especially important with an outfitter who asks for a security deposit to cover potential damage. You want to know the condition of what you're renting before you go. A good inspection also gives you leverage in buying used equipment. Know the retail price of a similarly designed new boat, and subtract the estimated wear on the craft. If you're game, try to negotiate a lower price. In the U.S., for information on testing or renting equipment in your region, contact the National Association of Canoe Liveries and Outfitters, P.O. Box 248, Butler, KY 41006 (telephone 606-472-2205).

SAFETY TIP Inspect your rental gear yourself to be sure it's in good shape. If it's not, don't take it!

Transporting Canoes

Once you've selected the appropriate gear, you've got to get it to water to begin your practice. Transporting a canoe can be made easy using an inexpensive foam block kit. The overturned canoe rests on four blocks; slits in the blocks allow the gunwales to nest in the foam. Tie the painter lines on the canoe to the front and back bumpers of your vehicle, and tie one or two lines over the canoe where it sits on the roof.

A canoe rack, though more expensive, makes it easier to tie the boat onto the car. You can reduce the expense by making a rack with brackets and lumber. Some paddlers have created racks wide enough to hold two canoes (about 75 to 80 inches, or 190 to 203 cm). You can also buy a rack designed specifically for holding a canoe. Some combination models accommodate other equipment, such as bicycles and skis, as well. You might as well become a triathlete! But let's begin with the canoeing.

3

CANOEING CORRECTLY

Now that you are properly equipped, you're ready to master canoeing's basic skills. First, you'll learn how to get the boat to the water and enter it in a balanced manner. Then it's time to practice the basic strokes and maneuvers that allow you to control the boat's movement. An orientation to rescue techniques rounds out your development as a capable canoeist.

This chapter enables you to get canoeing quickly and to develop your paddle sensitivity. For simplicity, I'll introduce a minimal number of strokes and maneuvers. After helping people learn to paddle for 15 years, I'm convinced that you need to begin with just enough strokes to get moving—and to feel right from the start what's happening between your body, the paddle, and the canoe. Later in your development you can continue to improve your paddling by exploring the many variations of the common strokes you'll learn here.

Make sure your rescue practice keeps pace with your practice of strokes and maneuvers. I worry about enthusiastic beginners I see who have no idea how to rescue themselves. This element is unfortunately overlooked by some new canoeists, but you'll be a more confident and responsible paddler if you develop the ability to rescue yourself and others. Every canoeist must take responsibility for his or her actions on water, because you can't rely on other people coming to your assistance.

Carrying the Canoe

I describe four specific kinds of canoe carrys on pages 36 and 37, but you should feel free to be flexible and creative with your carrys, since some boats may be heavy to new paddlers. There is no unwritten rule (except perhaps masochistic pride) that forces one or two people to carry a canoe. If necessary, use four or even six people, distributed evenly around the canoe to make the load lighter.

Paddles can be stowed in an upright canoe or carried by hand. In carrys where the canoe is overturned, you can stow paddles above the thwarts and hold them in place against the hull. Even easier, carry them to the water with your accessory gear.

SAFETY TIP To avoid straining your lower back, remember to always bend your legs when lifting a canoe off the ground. Lift with your legs!

Stabilizing the Canoe

Now that you've carried the canoe to the dock or shore, you must enter it with balance to avoid capsizing. Only one person should move in a canoe at a time to enhance stability. When entering from the shore, place the boat in the water, which makes it more stable than resting one end on land. Your partner can hold the canoe to stabilize it while you enter. After you've paddled awhile in a tandem canoe, you may want to change positions with your partner. Some paddlers prefer to paddle to shore to change positions. However, it may be necessary or quicker to change while afloat. Again, only one person should move at a time to enhance stability.

Follow the instructions on page 35 when entering a canoe or when changing positions to successfully keep your boat stable.

Keep The Canoe Stable

Entering

1. Grasping both gunwales, step into the canoe over the centerline.
2. Keep your weight low to lower your center of gravity.
3. Step along the centerline and slide your hands along the gunwales to move to your seat.

Changing Positions

1. The stern paddler crouches in the middle of the boat.
2. The bow paddler crawls backward over the partner, staying low and carefully balancing weight by sliding hands along the gunwales.
3. Once seated, the bow paddler should place paddle in the water to help stabilize the boat while the stern paddler finishes moving to the other seat.

Canoe Carrys

Solo Carry

Grab the gunwales at the middle of the canoe or slightly toward one end. Lift the boat and rest it on your thighs. One end of the canoe can remain on the ground for stability. Roll the boat upside down over your head, and let the midship thwart or the portage yoke rest against your shoulder blades. (A portage yoke is a thwart that is curved in the middle to fit around a person's neck.) You may have to slide the boat forward to reach this position, which lets one end of the canoe lift slightly off the ground.

Tandem Hand Carry

Partners stand at opposite ends of the canoe and on opposite sides to balance the weight. Grab the gunwales of the canoe near the deckplates, and lift the canoe. This carry works best for shorter distances. Four or six people, evenly spaced around the boat, can use this carry to lighten the load. Work in pairs on opposite sides of the canoe to balance the carry.

Tandem Portage Carry

Partners stand at opposite ends, but on the same side, of the canoe. With both hands, grab the gunwales on each side of the canoe, near the open spaces in front of the seats so that your head won't hit the seat during the carry. Use a 1-2-3 count to lift the canoe in unison, and rest it on your thighs. On another count, roll the canoe upside down over your head and rest the gunwales on your shoulders. Placing the taller person in front gives the best line of sight.

Tandem Shoulder Carry

This carry provides an unobstructed view for the front person. Follow the instructions for the tandem portage carry, but once the canoe is rolled overhead, the front person can move farther forward and lift the canoe onto one shoulder.

Sitting is the most comfortable position for paddling a canoe. Sit in the middle of the seat, and brace your legs or feet against the sides of the canoe. Some canoeists prefer to sit with legs outstretched, while others cross their legs for a stable stance.

If you are wary of a canoe's tippiness, you can kneel initially for more stability. Rest your buttocks against the edge of the seat and spread your knees apart. This position also may be desirable if wind and waves are building. Keeping your paddle in the water provides additional stability.

SAFETY TIP

Kneel in your canoe for greater stability in building waves or wakes from motorboats. Rest your buttocks against the seat and spread your knees wide.

Developing Stroke Skills

On the water you'll see many dabblers who can paddle a canoe, but they do it in an inefficient way that soon elicits complaints of tired arms. Modern canoeing has benefited in the last decade from a more scientific approach to sports in general, and we better understand the dynamics of efficient strokes. Important changes have also resulted from adapting strokes to the technology of lighter, more responsive boats.

Does canoeing seem to unduly fatigue your arms? In place of the traditional "arm-intensive" style of paddling, embrace a new "torso-intensive" style that uses your total body. Strive to paddle efficiently, and you'll be able to paddle longer and harder.

The Proper Paddle Grip

The key to efficient strokes is a firm but relaxed grip on the paddle. To avoid fatigue, clasp the paddle firmly for control but without tension. If your knuckles are white, release the paddle and shake out your hands. Then concentrate on grasping the paddle gently.

Check the distance between your hands by raising the paddle above your head. Your arms should form a 90-degree angle (or slightly less) at the elbow for maximum paddling power. Hands too close together provide too little leverage during strokes, and hands too far apart limit your reach away from the boat, which is important during turning strokes.

Maintain a consistent hold on the paddle with the top hand. This "grip" hand changes the angle of the paddle blade during turning strokes by

Finding the proper paddle grip.

rotating at the wrist. Do not indiscriminately swivel the grip in this top hand; that will interfere with your smooth execution of strokes. Your "shaft" hand, the one nearer the lower end of the shaft, guides the paddle through the water. During some turning strokes you will need to maintain a looser hold on the paddle shaft and let the paddle swivel in this shaft hand.

Paddling With Your Entire Body

Efficient use of your torso makes you a more successful canoeist. If you push and pull the paddle with your arms, the smaller arm muscles work

PADDLE EFFICIENTLY

1. Keep your arms comfortably straight and braced against the shaft.
2. Swivel or rotate your upper body to move the paddle into position.
3. Push down on the blade with your hands to insert it fully into the water and feel it "catch" solidly.
4. Unwind your torso to apply power through your straight arms against the paddle.
5. Avoid bending your arms, which absorbs your powerful thrust and forces the smaller muscles to push against the paddle.
6. Think of thrusting your hips toward the blade, which moves the boat dynamically toward the paddle.
7. Minimize bending forward at the waist to keep the boat from bobbing up and down.
8. Minimize dropping your torso to the side, which causes the canoe to dip.

Four Phases of a Stroke

Knowing the four distinct phases of a stroke can help you learn it quickly and execute it efficiently. I find this separation of the phases helpful, because new paddlers can slow down the action into meaningful parts rather than just seeing a blur of action. Let's examine the parts of a forward stroke to understand how

Catch

The beginning of the stroke where the blade is quickly inserted into the water. Place the blade fully in the water before you apply power against the blade. If you apply power too soon, it transfers ineffectively from your body to the blade. Sometimes an audible "thuck" sounds. Let the paddle slip quietly into the water.

Power

Rotating your torso transmits power to the blade. The first 6 inches (15 cm) of the stroke is the most powerful when your body is the most taut. Always rotate your torso so it faces the paddle throughout the stroke. This action keeps the stroke in front of your body where it is more powerful and reduces the potential for injury to your muscles and joints.

they blend together.

Think of the blade as having two "faces": the *powerface* is the side pressed against the water during a forward stroke; the *backface* is the side with no pressure against it. Knowing these two faces can help you orient the blade properly when you learn the canoeing strokes.

Exit

The paddle should leave the water with no resistance against the blade. Let it slide to the surface, then lift it cleanly from the water without "shoveling" water up, which forces the canoe down instead of forward.

Recovery

Return your paddle to the catch position by feathering the blade (keeping it flat and just above the water surface) to minimize wind resistance. You can also slice the blade with no resistance through the water back to the catch position. (Turn the blade 90 degrees from its position during the power phase.) A slice increases the boat's stability because your paddle stays "glued" to the water longer.

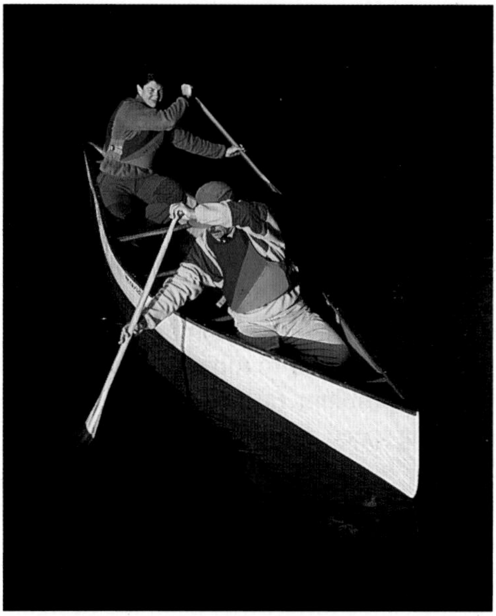

During an onside spin, tandem paddlers begin the draw stroke simultaneously . . .

. . . and slice the paddle underwater to return to the catch position.

circle or an *onside spin* because the paddles are on opposite sides, closer to the canoe ends and farther from the pivot point. The bow paddler sets the pace, and the stern paddler matches it. The stern paddler may have to lift the blade from the water earlier during the recovery to reduce water resistance. (See p. 46 for draw stroke instructions.)

The Pry Stroke

The *pry* moves the canoe strongly away from the paddle blade. It's a powerful, deep-water stroke because you use the canoe as leverage and ''pry'' the paddle off the gunwale. It moves a solo canoe sideways in an *offside sideslip*, while tandem canoeists use prys to pivot a canoe in an *offside spin*. The stroke dynamics remain the same, but the effect is different. In tandem canoeing, the canoe spins quickly in a circle because the positions of the paddles are on opposite sides, nearer the ends of the canoe and farther from the pivot point. (See pp. 47-48 for pry stroke instructions.)

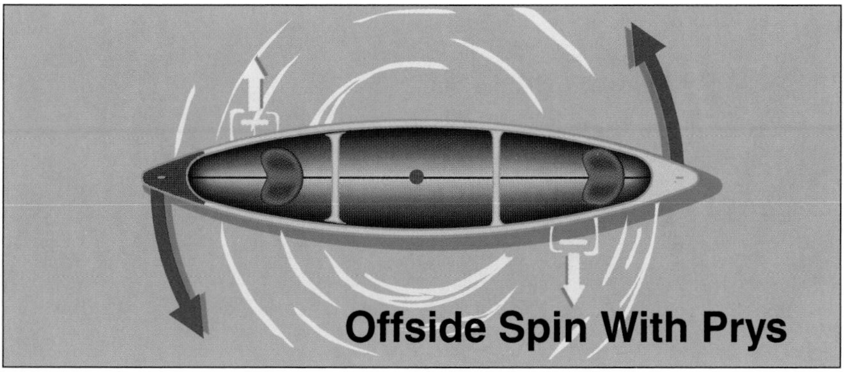

The pry stroke moves the canoe *away* from the paddle blade; here tandem pry strokes turn the boat quickly in a circle, or an *offside spin*.

Using a Draw and a Pry Together

Tandem canoeists can use different combinations of draw and pry strokes to move the boat sideways. For instance, the bow paddler can use a pry to move the bow away from the paddle while the stern paddler draws the stern toward the paddle. The two strokes used together move each end of the craft in the same direction. This move is called an *offside sideslip* because the boat is moving away from the bow canoeist's paddling side.

9. Recover the blade by changing the angle 90 degrees from the centerline to slice it back under the hull, rotating your thumb outward for the correct blade angle.
10. Realign the blade alongside the hull to continue the stroke.

Switching strokes moves the boat in the opposite direction in an *onside sideslip*, where the bow paddler performs a draw and the stern paddler a pry. (See p. 49.)

The Sweep Strokes

The *forward sweep* turns a canoe away from the paddle blade. The paddle is held parallel to the water, which helps to turn the boat off course. The *reverse sweep* pulls the canoe toward the blade, and it simply retraces the route of the forward sweep.

A solo paddler performs a *forward half sweep* in a 180-degree arc from one end of the boat to the other. It's important to begin and end the stroke near the canoe, but the paddle should be extended as far from the pivot point as comfortably possible at the midpoint of the stroke.

Tandem paddlers use a *forward quarter sweep* in a 90-degree arc from a position opposite their hips to the end of the canoe. Sweep strokes in a tandem boat are kept away from the pivot point, where the boat rests deeper in the water. The most important part of the stroke is near the curved ends of the canoe, where water resistance is less.

A tandem canoe spins when one partner uses a forward sweep and the other uses a reverse sweep. This strategy works especially well when a canoe is heavily rockered; the upturned ends provide little resistance against the water and the boat spins easily.

The offside sideslip: The bow paddler prepares for a pry stroke while the stern paddler readies the draw . . .

. . . and both paddlers slice their blades back to the catch.

MASTER THE REVERSE SWEEP FOR SOLO PADDLERS

1. Insert the paddle blade into the water near the stern, with the power-face facing the canoe.
2. Rotate your shoulders, aligning them with the blade.
3. Hold the paddle shaft parallel to the water.

4. Press the backface against the water.
5. Swivel your torso to move the canoe.
6. Begin to carve a 180-degree arc toward the bow.
7. Stern moves away from the paddle, bow swings toward it.

8. End the stroke just before the paddle strikes the bow.
9. Feather the blade low to the water back to the catch, powerface facing the sky.

Master the Forward and Reverse Sweep for Tandem Paddlers

Forward Sweep

Bow

1. Use the same dynamics as a solo paddler, except stop the stroke earlier.
2. Begin the stroke near the bow, carve a 90-degree arc toward the stern, and stop the stroke opposite your hip.

Stern

1. Begin the stroke opposite your hip.
2. Paddle a 90-degree arc until you reach the stern.

Reverse Sweep

Stern

1. Use the same dynamics as a solo paddler, except stop the stroke earlier.
2. Begin the stroke near the stern, carve a 90-degree arc toward the bow, and stop the stroke opposite your hip.

Bow

1. Begin the stroke opposite your hip.
2. Paddle a 90-degree arc until you reach the bow.

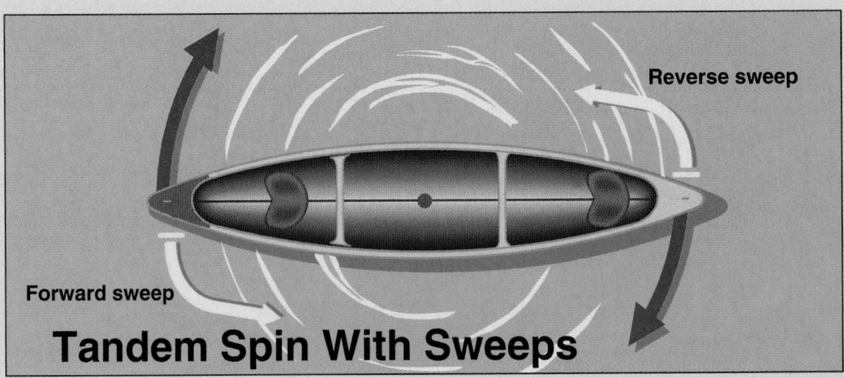

Tandem Spin With Sweeps

The Forward and the Back Strokes

Forget the old notions of a bent-arm, push–pull force against the paddle during the forward stroke. It's weak. Forget lunging forward by bending deeply at the waist and pulling your body back with the paddle, which porpoises the boat.

An efficient forward stroke combines a slight forward lean at the catch with rotation of the torso through the power and recovery phases. Think of your spine as a central axis; swivel your torso around it for a smooth stroke. Keep your arms comfortably extended as they grip the paddle, which creates an open square of torso, paddle, and arms. Using your skeletal structure this way creates a more powerful brace against the paddle. If you bend your arms at any time during the stroke, you close the square and reduce your power.

Remember to anchor the paddle firmly in the water at the catch. With the entire blade inserted in the water, you get more pressure against the water. Many beginners apply power too soon. You can actually hear the blade slipping in the water.

A touring forward stroke tends to be longer, with the paddle blade leaving the water just behind the hip. Shortening the stroke—stopping the blade before it reaches the hip—will quicken the tempo and increase power, which is effective against wind and waves and when you're racing. If you eventually want to try whitewater canoeing, practicing the short, quick forward stroke is important, because it gives you the power needed to handle fast current. The stroke is identical for all paddlers in solo and tandem canoes.

The back stroke strongly resembles the forward stroke—just reverse the process. The stroke begins at the hip and moves forward ahead of your body. Starting too far behind will result in excessive downward pressure against the blade, which inhibits backward momentum. Rotate your torso so it faces the paddle at the catch.

Remember to keep the paddle shaft perpendicular to the water surface with both hands over the water. The most common mistake with the back stroke is letting the paddle slide into a reverse sweep position, which turns the boat more than propels it backward.

The J Stroke

The J stroke, used by solo and tandem stern paddlers, keeps a canoe on a straight course. The J stroke needs to be efficient enough to keep the boat moving ahead, but it takes time to learn to do it smoothly without disrupting forward momentum. Many people quickly master one function or the other, but the real challenge is making them happen simultaneously.

PERFECT THE FORWARD STROKE

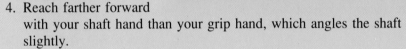

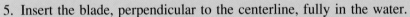

1. Keep the shaft perpendicular to the water surface, with both hands over the water to minimize any sweeping action.
2. Rotate your torso to slide the paddle into catch position, with the shoulder closest to the paddle (the shaft hand side) rotating forward.
3. Lean slightly forward at the catch for greater reach and power.
4. Reach farther forward with your shaft hand than your grip hand, which angles the shaft slightly.
5. Insert the blade, perpendicular to the centerline, fully in the water.
6. Keep your arms comfortably extended throughout all phases of the stroke.
7. Rotate your torso to apply power against the blade.

8. Thrust your hips forward.
9. Keep the path of the paddle parallel to the centerline throughout the power phase; don't follow the line of the gunwale.
10. Make sure the paddle exits the water just behind your hips.

11. Feather the blade back to the catch, low to the water, with the power-face facing the sky.

5. Slide the paddle shaft along the boat for more powerful leverage.
6. As the blade approaches your thigh, change the angle by rotating your grip hand away from your body and pointing your thumb away.
7. Slide the paddle into position at or just behind your hip, the powerface now facing away from the canoe.
8. Press the powerface outward to carve the J, with canoe and blade less than 12 inches (30-1/2 cm) apart.
9. Lever off the gunwale during the J phase for more power.

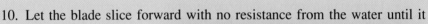

10. Let the blade slice forward with no resistance from the water until it rises to the surface.
11. Feather the blade back to catch, powerface facing the sky.

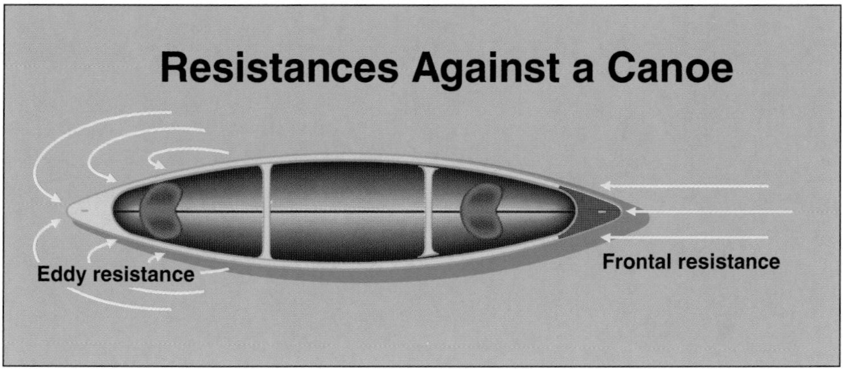

To maintain a straight course, it helps to understand the different kinds of water resistance.

end of the craft, because it slips more easily in the water. So if you paddle backward in a tandem canoe, the bow person is then in the eddy-resistance position and maintains the straight course with a reverse J.

Switch Paddling

Switch paddling is a good alternative to the J stroke for straight-ahead speed. Used by marathon racers and touring canoeists, this strategy eliminates a lot of corrective strokes, which reduce speed. It emphasizes forward strokes in a cadence that allows a synchronized switching of sides.

Tandem paddlers begin with forward strokes on opposite sides of the canoe. When the boat begins to veer off course, the stern paddler calls "hut," which is the signal to switch paddling sides. Without missing a beat, the canoeists change sides (which includes changing paddle grips) and continue to power-paddle forward. A regular cadence develops, and paddlers usually find themselves switching every 6 to 10 strokes, depending on boat design. The "hut" is actually called during the preceding stroke to give paddlers time to prepare for a unified switch.

Timing and a loud "hut" are crucial, especially in tippy racing canoes, because you risk a capsize if both paddlers end up stroking on the same side. Experienced racers tend to use bent-shaft paddles with this switch technique and only occasionally use corrective strokes.

This strategy must be a coordinated, synchronized switch between partners. When paddlers switch sides indiscriminately, they often fail to paddle in unison, which undermines momentum.

Use switch paddling if the J stroke proves to be frustrating, because it is guaranteed to get you moving across the water. It can also be an effective strategy in wind and waves during touring when you need a quicker tempo.

Putting it all Together

Does paddling in a straight line require constant J strokes? It shouldn't! To go straight, paddlers use maneuvers that combine forward, J, and forward sweep strokes. The more rockered the canoe (curved like a banana), the more often you're likely to use a J stroke. (That fact makes a good argument for choosing a touring canoe, which tracks straighter than recreational models.)

Try these practice exercises to develop your paddling skills:

Inside Circle Drill

Paddle in a circle by performing continuous J strokes. You'll be paddling on the side of the canoe that is to the inside of the circle. Leaning the canoe toward the paddle helps you execute the J effectively—you'll find that the circles will be tighter. After awhile, you can use forward sweeps and forward strokes to prevent the circle from tightening too much.

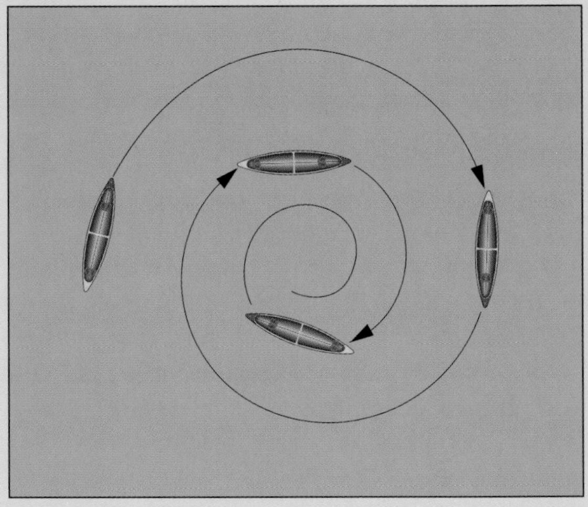

Quarter Moon Drill

Here you'll use the concept from the Inside Circle Drill to paddle a quarter-moon course. Pick a destination and angle your canoe so it's pointing 45 degrees away. Lean the canoe slightly to your paddling side, and execute continuous J strokes to begin the boat turning back toward the obstacle. As the canoe begins to swing toward the point, use forward strokes or sweeps to prevent the boat from overturning.

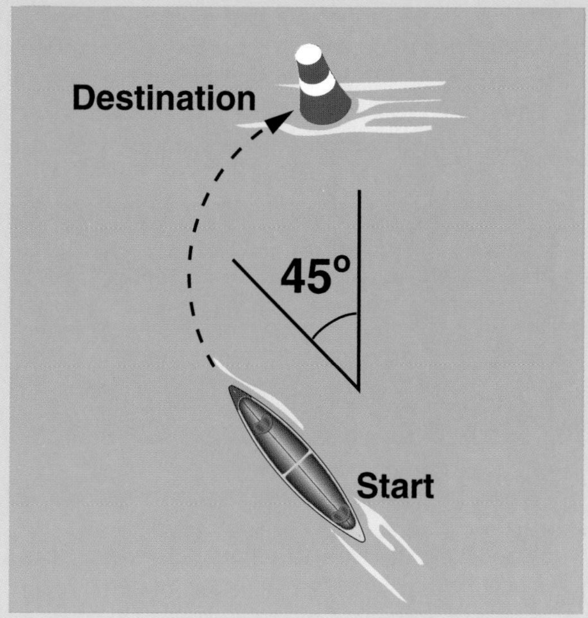

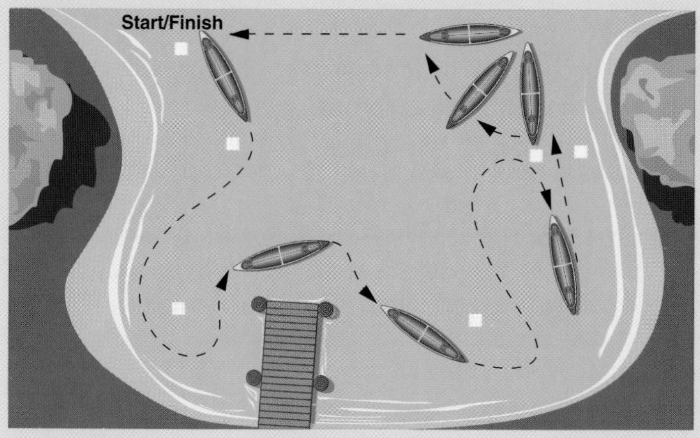

Multipoint Course

This drill combines paddling straight with turning. Use bobbers or major points on shore (docks, rocks, trees) as destinations. Paddle toward each point and turn at the point without an interruption in your speed. You can try the course paddling backward, too!

Developing Rescue Skills

Tipping over, an inevitable part of canoeing, can be caused by a paddler's losing balance, turbulent weather, or big wakes from other boating traffic. Always be prepared to swim. Every responsible paddler must master the principles of self-rescue and group rescue, and practice them regularly. Your training is incomplete until you have learned how to quickly rescue yourself, other paddlers, boats, and accessory gear.

RESCUE PRIORITIES

1. **People.** Wear your PFD. Take care of yourself first; then make sure your partner is okay.
2. **Canoes.** Stay with the highly visible boat, unless cold forces you to swim to shore for assistance.
3. **Accessory gear.** Store all gear in waterproof containers that will float. Save it last.

It can be difficult to remember rescue priorities in the confusion of a capsize. You should rescue people first, then a canoe, and then other gear. My students in an outdoor leadership program still talk about the whitewater capsize on an Adirondack canoe camping trip. One student was stranded on a rock, the boat was pinned, and the other paddler was trying to rescue his brand-new pack. A rescue bag trailing part of its line floated down to the paddler in the water and started wrapping around his legs. I began yelling, ''Let the pack go,'' and I got more forceful as he struggled with the heavy pack until it pulled him over. He finally returned to help rescue his partner and the canoe, but my command to ''let the pack go'' became a rallying point for the group. It became a way for the group to focus their priorities in many situations, not just an intense whitewater rescue!

People must come first in a rescue. They can suffer from the effects of hypothermia—a severe loss of body heat—even in warm summer weather. Cold water and wind can accelerate the loss of heat. You must get wet paddlers warm and dry as soon as possible. Packing extra dry, warm clothing is essential even in the summer.

Although it's important that your rescue skills be as well developed as your paddling, ultimately the key to your safety is good judgment. Strive to make informed, preventive decisions. Anticipate the impact of other canoeists, changing water conditions, worsening weather, and motorized boats and take responsible actions to prevent accidents.

Self-Rescue

At the heart of every rescue is self-rescue. You must be prepared to rescue yourself, because you cannot always rely on assistance from other people. If you're close to shore, you can swim with your canoe to shallow water. The canoe provides buoyancy if you need to rest, and it makes you easier to spot. If you're away from shore, you can roll the canoe over and reenter it. You can paddle a partially swamped canoe to shore—not easily but it can be done!

The *Capistrano flip* is an alternative method for two paddlers wearing lifejackets to quickly flip a boat (see p. 66). The Capistrano flip works best if the canoe is very buoyant; otherwise, the boat will remain partially swamped and you will have to bail it.

SAFETY TIP Know how to rescue yourself. Do not rely on others to assist you.

Group Rescue

You should be prepared to offer rescue assistance when traveling with a canoeing group. Group rescues are quicker and more efficient, which enhances the safety of all canoeists. You can get wet paddlers out of the water quickly, especially on cold days or in congested water.

If you are near shore, simply tow swimming paddlers to shore with their boats. Position your stern near the paddlers and hand them your stern line to hold. They should also hold the line attached to their canoe. As you paddle to shore, the swimmers should kick to help with the rescue.

The *canoe-over-canoe rescue* or *T rescue* is necessary when you are away from shore. It allows you to empty a canoe of water and rescue swimmers directly into it. One canoe can perform the rescue, which involves pulling the tipped-over canoe across the gunwales to empty it before rolling it and returning it to the water. However, an additional rescue boat can position itself along the first rescue canoe to stabilize the rescue. Other boats should remain clear of the rescue operation but can retrieve floating equipment.

The canoe-over-canoe rescue is an excellent method to practice with other canoeists. Children especially love to deliberately tip canoes and practice the rescues, which increases their skills tremendously. I've learned to plan more time for rescue ''play'' (otherwise known as practice) for kids' canoe trips, because some like it more than touring! Experienced paddlers can complete a rescue in 2 or 3 minutes.

KNOW THE CAPISTRANO FLIP

1. Position yourselves on opposite ends of the upturned canoe.
2. Duck under the boat into the air pocket, where you can talk easily.
3. Hold on to the gunwales; you may have to lift one gunwale to break the suction against the water surface.
4. On a 1-2-3 count, perform a scissors kick, simultaneously pushing up on the canoe to roll it upright.
5. Reenter the canoe, one at a time and from opposite sides: Use a scissors kick to propel yourself over the gunwale, tuck your shoulder, and roll into the canoe.

Be Prepared With The Canoe-Over-Canoe Rescue

1. The swimming paddler positions herself at the end of the overturned canoe.
2. The rescue boat positions itself at the other end, perpendicular to the swamped boat, forming a *T*.
3. The rescuers lift up on the overturned canoe as the swimmer pushes down on the other end to help break the suction.

4. The rescuers pull the other boat across their gunwales until it balances at midpoint. This position drains the water completely.
5. The swimmer moves to the rescue canoe and holds on.

6. The rescuers roll the other canoe over.

7. The rescuers slide the uprighted canoe back into the water, positioning it parallel to their boat and holding on to the gunwales to stabilize it.
8. The swimmer propels upward with a scissors kick, tucks her shoulder, and rolls into the canoe.
9. Once the swimmer is seated and has her paddle, the rescue boat can let go.

BASIC SKILLS CHECKLIST

Use this checklist to record the skills that you have mastered. The record will help focus your practice.

Balanced entry into the boat __
Stable sitting stance __
Ability to change positions __
Proper paddle grip __
Efficient use of the body __
Comfortably straight arms __
Rotation of the torso __
Efficient paddle strokes __
Effective power phase __
Effective recovery phase __
Basic maneuvers
  Spinning (pivoting) __
  Sideslipping __
  Following a straight course:
    Tandem __ Solo __

Strokes
  Forward: Tandem __ Solo __
  Back: Tandem __ Solo __
  Draw: Tandem __ Solo __
  Pry: Tandem __ Solo __
  Forward quarter sweep:
    Tandem __
  Forward half sweep: Solo __
  Reverse quarter sweep:
    Tandem __
  Reverse half sweep: Solo __
  J stroke: Tandem __ Solo __

RESCUE SKILLS CHECKLIST

Use this checklist to record your mastery of important self-rescue and group rescue skills.

Self-Rescue

Swimming in PFD __
Reentering a swamped canoe __
Swimming with canoe to shore __
Capistrano flip __

Group Rescue

Towing a swimmer and canoe __
Canoe-over-canoe rescue
  ''Victim'' practice __
  Primary rescue boat practice __
  Secondary rescue boat practice

It's important to receive periodic feedback about your canoeing skills to avoid developing inefficient or ''coping'' habits. Canoeing instructors and knowledgeable paddlers can analyze your progress and give a specific prescription for continued practice and improvement. Videotaped analysis is an invaluable tool, because you can connect what you see with what you feel while you paddle. Check with your local paddling school about this service.

I've been canoeing for 30 years and have viewed my whitewater performance on many videotapes; this has been enormously helpful, particularly each spring when I dust off my strokes. Every time I've explored a new aspect of canoeing, I've made an effort to get videotaped. It's often humbling, but inevitably highly motivating. First, it was my recreational marathon racing technique, and now it's freestyle canoeing. There's always room for improvement!

4

CANOEING FITNESS AND SAFETY

Inevitably in my canoe lessons there are beginners who are concerned they may not have enough strength to canoe. They're often fearful of holding back the partners with whom they are likely to paddle. But with canoeing they can let go of their fears, because it's accessible to people of all abilities. *You* determine the intensity and duration of your participation.

One of my ''breakfast canoe tours'' is a perfect example. The energetic among the canoeists in our crowd begin the tour at a point right near our house and paddle the 5 miles to the riverside diner. The sight-seeing canoeists, by contrast, drive to the restaurant, paddle half a mile around a nearby cove, do a little bird-watching, and wait for the other crew to round the river bend. Automatic canoe shuttle service, and everyone troops into breakfast together! Believe me, there really are no minimum fitness requirements (although the ample breakfasts do force one to consider a conditioning program).

Don't let a lack of conditioning prevent you or your companions from giving canoeing a try. The more important factor in canoeing is technique, and I always encourage beginners to strive to finesse the boat rather than muscle it around.

I've watched short, slight women with limited upper body strength take solo canoeing lessons and become excellent technical paddlers. They analyze the skills, fine-tune the moves, and ultimately paddle very efficiently. Consequently, their paddling often produces more speed than a bullish, technically poor approach.

You can use canoeing to improve your conditioning, but you can also condition your body beforehand to enhance your experience. Improved physical fitness will make canoeing more enjoyable, because you'll feel more energetic and be able to paddle longer distances without fatigue. You'll feel stronger and be able to handle routine tasks like carrying boats as well as unexpected difficulties like increasing winds. You'll also feel more flexible, and you'll be able to use your entire body to execute your strokes strongly and efficiently. Ultimately, your torso is likely to take on a streamlined shape from the effects of upper body rotation through the strokes.

Improved physical fitness has four major parts:

- *Cardiorespiratory fitness*—the heart's ability to pump blood and thereby deliver oxygen to your body.
- *Muscular strength and endurance*—the power and speed of your muscles, which directly affects the effectiveness of your paddling strokes (strength) and the ability to stroke repeatedly without fatigue (endurance).
- *Flexibility*—the ability of muscles and joints to stretch freely and smoothly without pain over a wide range of motion.
- *Body composition*—the level of body fat compared to the level of lean tissue, which can affect your flexibility and your health risks.

You can benefit from doing a two-step conditioning program designed for canoeists that mixes a variety of activities. Step 1 lets you determine your present level of fitness. Step 2 helps you build a program to get where you'd like to be. Monitoring your improvement helps motivate you to continue your conditioning.

Step 1: How Ready Is Your Body?

You must know yourself and analyze your participation in other recreational activities to assess your body's readiness for canoeing. Listen to your body carefully, and note any signs that may adversely affect your participation. Use the Prepaddling Health Check to determine your readiness.

PREPADDLING HEALTH CHECK

1. Do you ever feel faint or have spells of severe dizziness?
2. Do you have a history of heart trouble or high blood pressure?
3. Do you have any joint problems, such as arthritis, that could be aggravated by canoeing?
4. Do you have any muscular problems, such as lower back strain, that could be aggravated by canoeing?
5. Are you taking any prescription medications?
6. Have you recently been treated for any physical condition that may affect your participation?

If you answer yes to any question in the health check, you should consult your doctor before canoeing. An instructor is also likely to ask these questions on a medical report form that you fill out before a lesson. The answers are held in confidence, but they help the instructor prepare adequately for individual medical needs—both in first aid preparedness and in the progression of activities, which should be tailored to individual needs. To plan properly, you should also be aware of the medical histories of everyone when you paddle with friends.

Determining Your Cardiorespiratory Fitness

Recreational canoeing is not a high-intensity activity, so your cardiorespiratory fitness isn't likely to be challenged greatly in the beginning. (That comes later if you become obsessed by racing and want to train 600 to 1,000 hours a year like national class canoeists!) If you can't run a record-pace footrace or swim a freestyle race in championship time, you'll still do just fine in canoeing.

However, cross-over benefits from other sports that emphasize the upper body can prepare you for canoeing. If you cross-country ski or swim regularly (2 or 3 times a week), your transition to canoeing will be easier because your torso and arms will be more fit. If you use a rowing machine, you are already using many of the muscles specific to paddling. A full day of canoeing should be within your abilities at the beginning.

Bicycling, jogging, and walking improve your overall cardiorespiratory fitness, but they do little for your upper body. If one of these activities is your primary cardiorespiratory exercise, recognize that it may be wise to canoe for only a portion of a day at the beginning, until you get a clearer sense of your upper body strength.

If you have a limited history of participation in other recreational activities, plan a shorter introduction to canoeing—perhaps several hours or half a day, with plenty of options for stopping sooner if you need to. One of the nicest benefits of canoeing is that it can be done at a slow pace, which is why it appeals to many people with limited exposure to the outdoors. Even though I do a lot of backpacking, mostly on cross-country skis, I still prefer canoeing because I'd rather let the canoe carry the weight of my gear during the day.

Determining Your Muscular Strength and Endurance

You don't want to test your strength and endurance for canoeing by leaving on a day tour and discovering by noon that your muscles are unhappy. Those dormant muscles promise to be in extreme distress when you reach the take-out at the end of the day. Your frame of reference for judging your readiness is again your participation in other recreational activities.

Match the duration of your initial canoeing experiences to the length of your participation in other activities, or plan a slightly shorter first venture. If you can cross-country ski for a day, then you should be able to canoe for a day. If you can swim nonstop for an hour, then you can canoe for at least several hours, because you can stop more frequently in a boat. Remember that it's better to stop too soon, wanting more, than to go too long and pay the price with sore muscles.

One poor test of your strength might be whether or not you can carry a canoe! Make sure you get a light boat, because then it won't stop you from paddling. Or get a few friends to help carry a heavier one. Some of my favorite trips are with 50- and 60-year-old women new to canoeing. Most can't carry the boats easily (it becomes a group project), but they paddle happily for 4 or 5 hours and sleep well that night!

Finding Out How Flexible You Are

The range of motion in your upper body is the biggest factor affecting your beginning paddling. Your torso needs to follow the blade during strokes for enhanced power. If you neglect to use the large, powerful muscles of your torso as you execute strokes, then your smaller, weaker arm muscles, which will tire more easily, are doing the work. Think of your trunk muscles as boosters; they drive additional power to the arms to make you a stronger paddler.

Using torso rotation also keeps your blade in front of your body and protects against injury. A shoulder dislocation is possible (although infrequent) if your arms move over your head and behind your body during a stroke. Although limited flexibility doesn't stop you from paddling, it does affect the efficiency of your strokes. Greater range of motion will let you be a more powerful paddler.

CHECK YOUR FLEXIBILITY

1. Lay your paddle on the ground and straddle it.
2. Stretch out your arms, rotate your torso, and try to align your arms with the line of the paddle.
3. Record the degree of your flexibility, and use it as a reference during your conditioning program to determine your improvement.

Arms move beyond parallel alignment? You are very flexible.
Arms aligned with paddle? You are flexible.
Arms cannot reach parallel alignment? You are somewhat inflexible.

ARM CIRCLES Loop the surgical tubing around a tree at shoulder level. Hold the loop at the other end, and move away until you feel a comfortable tension. Swing your arm slowly in small, then large circles in both directions. Switch arms.

ARM CIRCLES

PUNCHES Lie on your back, holding hand weights. Alternating hands, punch directly upward.

SIDE LIFTS Stand holding hand weights with arms straight down at your sides. Lift the weights outward in an arc to shoulder level and back down.

PULL-UPS Stabilize the pole over two sturdy armchairs. Men lie on the back on the floor and grab the bar from beneath, using a straight-leg position. Women use a bent-knee position with feet flat on floor. Take hold of the bar and pull up, bringing the chest as close to the bar as possible. Then lower yourself slowly until your arms are fully extended.

PULL-UPS

DIPS With legs either bent or straight (straight legs require more arm strength), hold the edge of a chair, and lower yourself straight down and back up.

DIPS

Stretching Your Muscles

Stretching is a multipurpose activity! You can stretch for the sake of improving flexibility, or you can use these exercises during your warm-ups to ready your muscles for activity or during your cool-downs to reduce stiffness and soreness.

To stretch effectively, move slowly to the point of slight tension. Breathe regularly, exhaling with exertion and inhaling as you return to your starting position. Hold a stretch for 15 seconds, then repeat it three to five times.

TORSO TWISTS Stand with feet shoulder-width apart and a paddle resting on your shoulders. Rotate your upper body slowly and hold the stretch at its farthest point. Repeat in the opposite direction.

BENT TORSO TWISTS With paddle resting on your shoulders, bend forward at the waist. Twist your torso until one hand points toward the opposite foot. Hold the stretch. Alternate to the other side.

BENT TORSO TWISTS

OVERHEAD REACH Interlace your fingers above your head with palms facing up. Reach up to stretch the arms, shoulders, and upper back.

C STRETCHES Loop the surgical tubing around an obstacle (e.g., a sturdy pole) at your side. Bend the other direction until the inside of your body creates a C. Feel and hold the stretch in the opposite side. Now face the other direction and repeat.

C STRETCHES

BACK-UPS Lying on your stomach, lift your head and one leg at the same time. Avoid arching your neck back. Repeat using the other leg. Now bend your legs, hold on to both feet, and lift up.

WRIST CIRCLES Rotate your wrists to perform hand circles. Keep your fingers extended to relax your hands. Repeat in the other direction.

SHOULDER HANG Hang the tubing above your head around a tree limb and hold onto both loops. Bend forward at the waist to reach a 90-degree bend, and lean back against the tubing. Back up until you feel the pull in both shoulders. Then stretch each shoulder individually by hanging from each arm.

SHOULDER HANG

SHOULDER REACH Hold a pole upright with palm out. Feel the stretch in the shoulder, arm, and wrist. Gradually turn your body away to feel more pressure. Finish by turning your head away. Don't push against the pole with your arm.

SHOULDER REACH

ELBOW PULL Raise one arm above your head, then bend it so your hand is behind your head. With the other hand, grasp your elbow and pull down and back. Gradually apply more pressure to increase the stretch.

ELBOW PULL

HIP-TORSO STRETCH Stretch one leg in front of you, and cross the other leg over it at the knee. Twist your torso away from the outstretched leg. Use your arm to press against the knee. Repeat on the other side.

HIP-TORSO STRETCH

Improving Your Body Composition

Canoeing regularly will improve your body composition (your percentage of body fat) just as any regular aerobic activity will. If you paddle once or twice a week during the warm months, you will soon feel a difference in the flexibility and muscle tone in your torso.

Canoeists can burn 150 to 720 calories an hour, depending on the intensity of their paddling. If you are touring slowly and stop often to relax, your energy expenditure will be lower. Canoe racers hit the higher end of the scale, often for 2- to 3-hour periods or longer during marathon races.

After canoeing almost daily for 5 years, I started graduate school, which consumed my time and prevented me from paddling much at all for a year. I was amazed at the softening of my abdomen and my loss of flexibility (as well as some attitude problems from being unable to paddle!). I eventually resumed a more normal schedule and regained my earlier level of fitness, but not without some struggles.

Commit yourself to your conditioning program. And be ready to run back to it if other parts of your life interfere periodically. It enhances your canoeing enjoyment and safety, and you are less likely to suffer injuries. The next step is addressing other factors that affect your paddling safety.

Basic Guidelines for Safe Touring

In my canoeing dreams, the scenery is always spectacular, drenched in sun and warm breezes, and the paddling is effortless. We always get underway early in the day, stay on schedule, and leave nothing behind (particularly the gourmet lunch about which I fantasize from my first graceful step into the canoe). Unfortunately, real paddling trips don't always fit the dream tour.

Sometimes your brother forgets his PFD, a friend of a friend with a real party mentality arrives with a case of beer, the wind starts to build before lunch—the lunch that you discover made it only as far as the back porch. Some factors are within your control, but others are beyond it. We know the weather can't be controlled, but we can count on its perversity and be prepared for it.

You need good judgment to paddle safely and responsibly each time you embark on a canoe tour. Unfortunately, the number of canoeing accidents has risen with the activity's increased popularity. Each canoeist has a personal responsibility to participate safely for his or her own sake and for the safety of others in a canoeing group.

Four major factors have contributed to recorded canoeing accidents: not wearing a PFD, alcohol consumption, cold water, and inexperience. Avoid these pitfalls; paddle wisely when you're ready to explore local waterways. It's as much a part of paddling well as efficient technique.

Begin with an honest appraisal of your paddling ability, and choose your route wisely. Tailor the location to your skills, which include paddling and rescue. You may want the security of a protected pond or ocean harbor or a narrow river with nearby banks rather than a large, exposed body of water. A realistic self-evaluation makes your early experiences pleasant.

Don't choose rivers beyond your ability, especially those that include whitewater sections. I can guarantee you'll get more ''experience'' than you want. I admit to having little patience with ''we almost died but we survived'' stories (especially magazine accounts), because the paddlers usually got into the situations because of their own poor judgment.

Try shorter distances at first if you are unsure of your strength and endurance and if you plan to travel with children. I discovered the hard way that my idea of a great tour (stunning scenery) isn't a child's top choice (lots of places to stop, explore, swim, and eat). To me, 4 to 6 miles is a moderate tour; to a young child, it's an eternity.

Be aware of alternate routes and exit points in case of fatigue or emergency. The best lakes and rivers have several points of access, often landing sites developed by the town or state. Use river reference guides or topographical maps to check for additional points, like bridge crossings or roads that swing near the river. Being familiar with this information before your trip helps you make a more informed choice and react better in case of an emergency.

I once planned a 4-mile canoeing trip for a group of junior high school kids. I'd done the trip many times with other groups, sometimes in half a day. But this group was particularly unathletic, and we'd covered only a mile by lunch. I changed our exit point rather than flog them down the river, and they had a great time. My point is this: Have alternatives, and be flexible enough to change your plans. It keeps you out of trouble.

Be respectful of private property when you're choosing your route. Get permission from landowners if you need to cross their land or want to stop on their property for lunch. Too many canoeists abuse this common courtesy, and more landowners are posting signs on their land against trespassing. Don't even consider camping overnight on someone's property unless you have permission. A goal of every canoeist should be to preserve public access to our waterways.

Simple courtesies can get results. A popular take-out on the West River in Vermont had been closed by the landowner, so the paddling grapevine reported, but my trip itinerary for a group of older women made that point our best exit. I knocked on the landowner's door a day before the trip and was given permission, because I'd been polite enough to make personal contact ahead of time, explain the trip, and promise not to leave trash behind. He still closes his land to other parties.

On the day of your tour, check the weather and note the likely wind conditions. Rain needn't stop a canoe tour, although a storm with thunder and lightning should. (I like a gentle, warm rain myself—it keeps the crowds away.) But a canoeist's major enemy is the wind, which tends to build midday. Consider paddling early or late in the day when conditions are usually (although not always) calmer. A solo canoe trip can be a disaster in wind, and you'll do one only once before you tire of the windmill effect on your boat. I have watched solo canoeists in gusty winds struggle to make it back to shore. Choose water with sheltered bays and bends.

Bring extra warm, dry clothing in a waterproof container, even if the morning sky is cloudless. You are guaranteed to attract dark, stormy clouds if you leave extra clothing behind—the *Farmer's Almanac* doesn't mention this fact, but it's a confirmed New England weather principle. Remember to dress for the water temperature rather than the air temperature in case you find yourself swimming.

Personal flotation devices weren't really designed to pad your canoe seat or to be used as cushions by nonpaddling companions, although I've seen lots of situations where this seemed to be the primary function. Wearing your PFD is wise, because capsizing can be chaotic, and you'll have flotation to aid in rescuing yourself or helping a panicky partner. Cold water can weaken even the strongest swimmers—they may not see the need to wear one, but a properly fitting PFD can save your life.

Be properly equipped for your canoe tour: all equipment in good repair, extra paddles stowed where easily accessible, and a first aid kit quickly available. Pack hearty meals with a generous supply of beverages. An exercising adult often drinks 2 liters of water to stay properly hydrated, and some people need up to 4 liters. Water is especially important when you canoe on hot days, because dehydration combined with glare from the sun can cause headaches. Drink before you become thirsty.

Pack out all trash—yours as well as the unclaimed goodies of others. Many motorboaters, paddlers, and anglers haven't adopted the low-impact ethic. Trash clutters the banks of many popular rivers and picnic and camping sites, which is unsightly and downright dangerous in some instances. Broken glass and fishhooks are common hazards for canoeists.

Take extra trash bags on trips, and make it a habit to clean up any area you use. I turn kids' trips into low-key scavenger hunts to see who can find the most exotic stuff. They get the message very quickly and are usually quite indignant at the volume they collect. (I don't dare list some of the better finds.) If every canoeist could set this example with her or his paddling group, we'd make major strides in cleaning up our shores.

EARTH WATCH Keep river and lake shores clean. Pick up litter, even if it was left by others.

Do not consume alcohol or other drugs while paddling. They dull your reflexes and judgment, which can be crucial if you capsize. In fact, drug consumption can undermine your balance and encourage tipping over. In the worst scenarios, canoeists suffer a gasp reflex when they tumble into cold water and drown after inhaling water.

Paddle in a group to enhance safety and ease of any rescue. Don't paddle alone unless you are confident that you can rescue yourself and your gear. Three to four boats is a manageable number—plenty of help for canoe-over-canoe rescues and just enough to maintain a cohesive group.

The major problem with traveling in a large group is the inevitability of separation. People paddle at different speeds, and as the boats drift apart, communication with all members becomes a problem in the event of an emergency. It can also be a simple matter of personal comfort and happiness. The weakest paddlers often become the tail-end boats as the trip progresses, when they might benefit physically and psychologically from a midtrip switch to stronger partners. It's wise to divide a large party into smaller groups for easier travel.

Establish organizational guidelines for a tour. Identify a lead boat to head the pack and a sweep boat to bring up the rear; all remaining boats paddle between these two. Decide whether you'll maintain voice-contact or visual-contact limits; some group members might prefer the security and sociability of staying within voice contact. Others like the solitude possible within the broader range of visual contact.

The key point here is keeping sight of the boats in your party. A commonly accepted rule of travel among canoeists is that you keep track of the boat in front of you and, most importantly, the one behind. If the canoe following falls behind or stops, then you stop and wait for it to catch up. This strategy should trigger a chain reaction among all boats to the front of the pack, until the lead boat has also stopped.

Finally, establish a reasonable schedule based on your route research, and follow it. Experienced canoeists can paddle about 3 miles (or nearly 5 km) in an hour; beginners cover considerably less distance. A mile can take some groups most of a morning. Be conservative at the beginning with short trips, and allow plenty of time to finish your tour before dark. Remember to add time for a relaxing lunch stop and rest breaks. Keep track of the time it takes to cover the mileage, and you'll have an accurate gauge for how far you can go.

My longest paddling day totaled 72 miles (116 km) on the fast-flowing Thelon River in sub-Arctic Canada, and I don't ever care to repeat the experience. It took us 12 hours. We were making up mileage that we had lost to 4 days of incredible winds when we couldn't move from our camp. Although we had figured bad-weather days into our schedule, the weather had been atrocious that summer. Even the best-calculated plans can go awry; it's important to plan thoroughly for a canoe tour and use judgment based on skills and knowledge to execute or change the original plan.

10 COMMANDMENTS FOR TOURING SAFELY

1. Don't choose rivers beyond your ability.
2. Choose your routes wisely; try shorter distances first.
3. Be respectful of private property.
4. Dress properly for the activity and the weather.
5. Wear a properly fitting PFD.
6. Be properly outfitted with equipment in good repair.
7. Do not consume alcohol or other drugs.
8. Paddle with a support party.
9. Establish organizational guidelines for the tour.
10. Establish a reasonable schedule and stick to it.

SAFETY TIP Alcohol dulls your judgment and increases your heat loss. Save the rum for after the run.

5

THE BEST PLACES TO CANOE

Now that you have learned the fundamentals of paddling, you need opportunities to refine your skills and to explore the wealth of waterways in every part of the world. Canoe travel can be as accessible as a quiet local stream or a nearby weekend getaway and as exotic as an extended paddling vacation in foreign geography or topography. But the common thread is the reward of canoe touring that provides you with a new perspective on travel. Getting there can be as important and as enjoyable as arriving at a particular destination.

The distance is your choice. Some of my favorite excursions have been barely half a mile long. A bald eagle reintroduction campaign in the state of Massachusetts has been so successful that a pair have nested on an island near my house on the Connecticut River. I've spent hours with other canoeists of all ages, watching the antics of young eaglets around the massive nest as they learn to fly.

Watching Wildlife

Observing wildlife from your canoe can be magical. You'll be able to see amazing sights if you show proper respect.

1. Paddle quietly, without talking as you approach.
2. Don't flash your paddle blades. Feather them low to the water or slice them beneath it so reflected sun doesn't startle the animals.
3. Keep a respectful distance; your presence can adversely affect animals and may startle some, particularly moose, into charging.
4. Stay at least 100 feet (30-1/2 m) from nesting sites; use binoculars to get a close-up view. If parents or young act distressed, move farther away. Be ready to leave the scene entirely.

Trip timing is also your choice. Some of my most special outings are full-moon tours, when the river is serene and bathed in shadows. You can count on having the water to yourself at midnight, and in New England we commonly hear owls and coyotes in the surrounding hills as we glide silently along the river. Plan an overnight trip on a full-moon weekend, and I guarantee a memorable experience for your group.

The key to a safe, enjoyable trip is planning. Whether the trip is one day or several, you need to consider a number of details to be well organized. My family kids me about my lists and tells me I act like an overgrown camp counselor, but I rarely forget anything important.

Part of this obsession stems from my experience planning 2-month canoe trips in northern Canada on the rivers that flow into the Arctic Ocean. I use standard checklists for everything—from menu planning to a ''spare-and-repair'' kit to my personal gear—because, when the float plane drops us 500 miles from any civilized point, we're stuck with what we've got. It's a sobering and exciting feeling. I have a friend who forgot the stove fuel for a similar Barren Lands trip, and the group had to wait for another plane to deliver it. Being caught without essential items can ruin your trip.

Preplanning begins with research about your canoeing route and the environment or country. Specific paddling information is often hard to find; popular tourist guides can be helpful, even if incomplete. Many countries have national canoeing associations that can offer information and advice about their recreational paddling opportunities (see a partial list in the appendix). Tourist agencies in a country are another source of general boating information, but be sure to ask specifically about canoeing or they may send only motorboating details.

Licenses and permits are important to research, because public access to rivers varies greatly between countries and within regions of a country.

Check with local, regional, or national river and park authorities to determine whether permits are necessary, and secure appropriate permission before embarking. This courtesy helps to prevent further restrictions to access as canoeing becomes more popular.

Permission from private landowners may also be necessary for access and egress; some may charge a fee. Getting permission in advance is wise, and I've found that a phone call or visit pays great dividends with many landowners whose property has been abused. Please treat landowners with respect and courtesy to maintain access for all paddlers.

Permits and fees may be required for camping, and reservations are often necessary in popular designated canoe areas. Don't overlook this detail, or you can be left without a home for the night. In Europe, primitive camping with landowner permission is a good option to explore. Most local residents are very receptive to canoeists who practice low-impact camping.

TOURING TIP Check your paddling plan with local authorities. Permits may be required for paddling and camping.

Knowledge of the local climate is crucial. Determine the water and air temperature for the season so you pack appropriate clothing and equipment. Also find out the area's prevailing winds, particularly on large bodies of water, to anticipate the safest shores for travel. Check rainfall and headwater conditions to determine whether rivers are likely to rise swiftly.

When I paddled the Rio Grande through Big Bend National Park in Texas during a very warm January, we had to be extremely careful about rainstorms. The arroyos—water-carved gulleys—act as big drains to funnel run-off into the river, and heavy rain can create flash flooding. It influenced our choice of campsites and sharpened the group's cloud watching to forecast weather changes.

Water levels can be an issue in another way. Free-flowing rivers are increasingly rare, and hydroelectric generating facilities or lock operators may control the water levels, which often fluctuate daily. Published river guides offer advice on which seasons and water levels are best for particular rivers. You can check daily with dam operators and local outfitters to find out a river's height.

Investigate whether you should bring your own equipment to have the right gear or if you can rely on local rentals. Canoeing is an integral part of North America's heritage, and rental and replacement equipment is generally easy to find here. It may be less available in other countries, where kayaking and sea kayaking may be more popular than canoeing.

You may need to bring your own gear as well as spare equipment, because replacements could be difficult to find.

Don't trust the water of urban rivers and lakes; carry potable water. Away from the cities, chemically treat or boil all water from lakes and rivers to prevent intestinal problems. The headwaters of New Zealand rivers and northern Canadian rivers are considered pure and drinkable. When in doubt, be conservative.

Minimum-Impact Canoe Travel

All outdoor travelers need to respect the fragility of our environment and be committed to minimizing their impact. We need to leave sites as we'd like to find them: as pristine as possible. That may mean cleaning up someone else's trash to restore the site. As more people travel outdoors, it's not unusual to find evidence of their passage in ill-conceived fire pits, remnants of toilet paper, and hatchet lines in the trees where live boughs have been cut for firewood.

EARTH WATCH Follow your own Adopt-a-Shore program. Leave your campsite cleaner than you found it.

Please consider that the impact along rivers and lakes is concentrated on the shoreline, often within a narrow corridor of several hundred feet or less. Where brush is dense, it's difficult to get farther away from the water, and it may be best to use campsites already cut from the forest. In canoeing the St. John River in northern Maine, we discovered the only campsites to use are the well-used existing ones, which are generally too close to the water. Hacking out a new site would be needlessly destructive.

Although general guidelines for low-impact travel are useful, it's helpful to remember that they are guidelines, not commandments. The special environment of a particular region may suggest a variation. For instance, a generally accepted guideline is that all personal hygiene be done 200 feet (61 m) from a water source to avoid contaminating the water with soap and food and waste residues. However, the Maine Island Trail Association recommends that all washing be done below the tide line, because the ecosystem of a small island can't handle the remnants left by many paddlers. Check with local agencies to find out what the staff recommend along your proposed route.

EARTH WATCH Protect fragile shorelines. Use existing trails, and tread carefully to prevent erosion.

Use common sense bolstered by an awareness of what is right for the ecology of your site. If you guard against the trap of laziness, you'll make good decisions and convince other paddlers to embrace this philosophy. The camp you leave behind should be a welcome site to the next visitors.

One additional reminder: All recreational enthusiasts have a right to enjoy our lakes and rivers. Respect especially the rights of anglers with whom you'll share the waterways, and stay well away from their lines.

TEN GUIDELINES FOR CANOEING RESPONSIBLY

1. Pack out all trash, including toilet paper and food leftovers. Never bury it.
2. Use existing trails rather than creating new ones.
3. Minimize riverbank erosion by not wearing heavy boots.
4. Stay within the boundaries of existing hardened sites, or choose a durable surface like sand or the forest floor for your tent.
5. Use a campstove for cooking, and choose a sandy or rock site where you're unlikely to ignite the leaf matter or grass.
6. Build a campfire only if a pit already exists and enough deadwood is nearby. Burn the wood thoroughly, and extinguish the fire completely.
7. Do not cut live boughs from trees. They don't burn well and you strip the trees.
8. Do all personal hygiene 200 feet (61 m) from any water source.
9. Keep all foods, soaps, insect repellents, and sunscreens out of the water supply.
10. Keep pets under control, and don't camp near animal dens or nests.

Traveling With Children

Canoeing is one of the better and easier ways to introduce children to the outdoors. When I think of backpacking with kids, I remember my father carrying my 5-year-old sister up over the harder sections in the

Presidential Range of the White Mountains in New Hampshire. He had a pack on his back, so he held my sister in front, which he was willing to do to get the whole family hiking. On a canoe trip, the boat carries the weight, which seems much more sensible to me!

Don't confuse your goals with kids' goals. To be remotely successful, trips with children should be planned for them, not for you. I have friends who liked the infant years best—their kids slept blissfully in the canoe, even through rolling waves. The preschool years are a little more difficult, because many toddlers become restless with the confinement. My brother-in-law built a modified crib with a high railing for the midsection of his canoe. This nifty arrangement let his children move around and nap on comfortable pads (but please note that they owned a very stable canoe!).

Last summer my husband and I paddled on a lovely coastal Maine stream with friends who have a 2-year-old daughter. They were prepared to go through the preparations, including packing a few favorite dolls and stuffed animals, which took longer than the canoeing itself. (They are thrilled with any journey longer than an hour.) Their daughter loves to be dangled over the side of the canoe; they hold her by the back of her lifejacket and use a great doughnut-dunking technique. But she has her limits with confinement, and they have their limits with arm strength. Short trips are the norm with kids this young.

A solo carry . . . with a little help. Photo by Bob Krist/Leo de Wys.

TOURING TIP When touring with kids, treat your canoe like a playground. Make it a fun (but safe) place to be.

Children who are a little older like canoe trips with lots of stops for exploring and swimming. A good strategy is combining a canoe trip with a short nature hike or a stop at a sandy beach or ledge. When children are ready to put paddle to the water, they'll tell you. But be prepared to paddle alone while they rest or sightsee. In fact, count on doing most of the paddling, which means that you should feel comfortable with your skills. If you like sunbathing, you'll be a real hit with many adolescents; traveling with teenagers is when I feel most like a gondolier. Forget getting anywhere quickly; relax and shift into low gear.

After you've gathered your group, it's time to select a route that they'll enjoy. The following sections highlight interesting excursions for shorter and longer tours that will tempt you to explore a variety of regions by canoe.

United States Getaways

Because the canoe played a major role in the exploration of the United States, access to many waterways has been supported as a public right. As a result, a wealth of canoeing opportunities are available, many of them in national and state parks designed specifically for canoeing.

The last two decades have seen amazing reverses in industrial pollution of American rivers and a renewed commitment to the protection of waterways, particularly through the National Wild and Scenic Rivers system. The commitment to preserving American waterways has never been greater. Certainly the size of the country provides an opportunity to experience an unusual diversity of river ecosystems—from placid southern streams to the jewel-like network of lakes and rivers along the northern border.

THE NORTHEAST

Exploring major rivers like the Connecticut and the Merrimac and their tributaries leads you into a beautiful countryside full of Native American and colonial history. I paddle almost daily on the Connecticut in spring, summer, and autumn, watching deer swim across the river and red-tailed hawks soar overhead.

Thoreau's account of "A Week on the Concord and Merrimac" is an intriguing companion on a river float. My first canoe overnight trip was

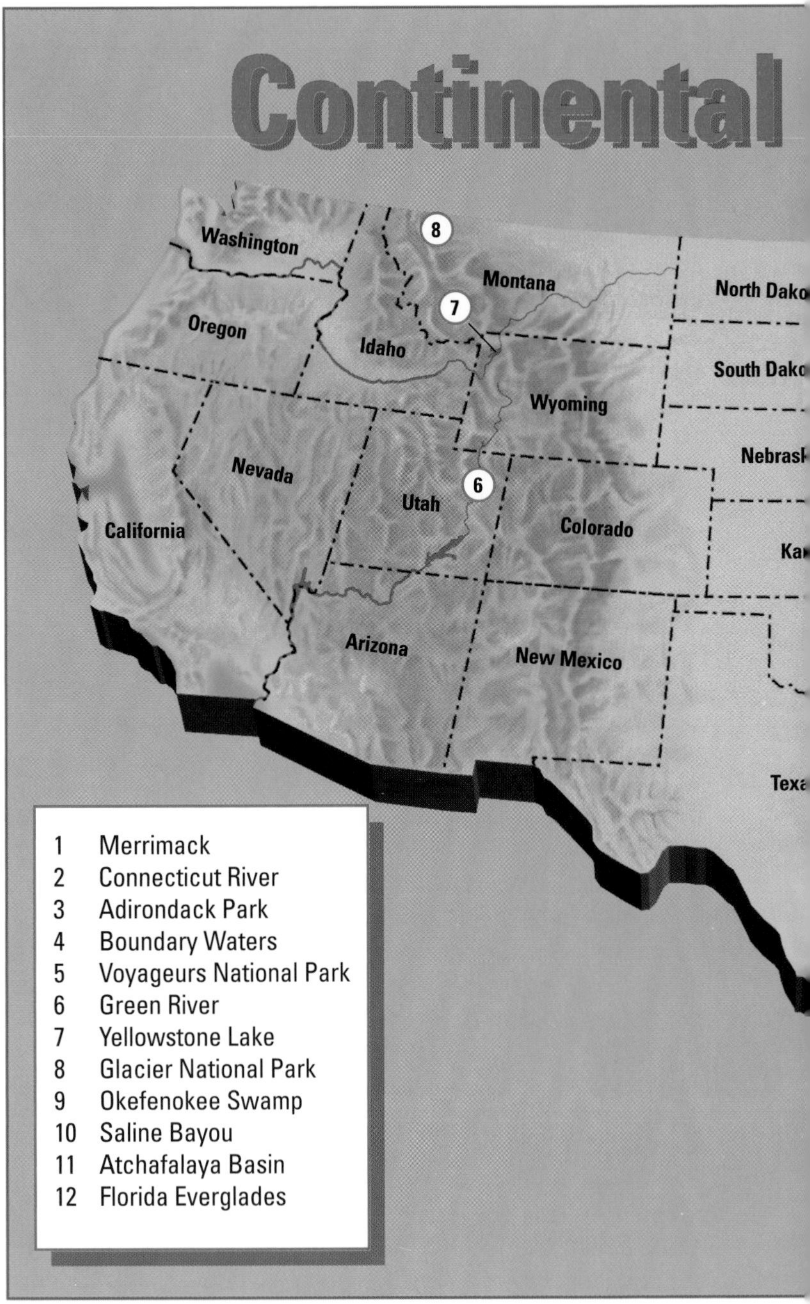
Continental
Washington
Oregon
Idaho
Montana
North Dako
South Dako
Wyoming
Nebrask
Nevada
Utah
Colorado
California
Ka
Arizona
New Mexico
Texa
8
7
6
1 Merrimack
2 Connecticut River
3 Adirondack Park
4 Boundary Waters
5 Voyageurs National Park
6 Green River
7 Yellowstone Lake
8 Glacier National Park
9 Okefenokee Swamp
10 Saline Bayou
11 Atchafalaya Basin
12 Florida Everglades

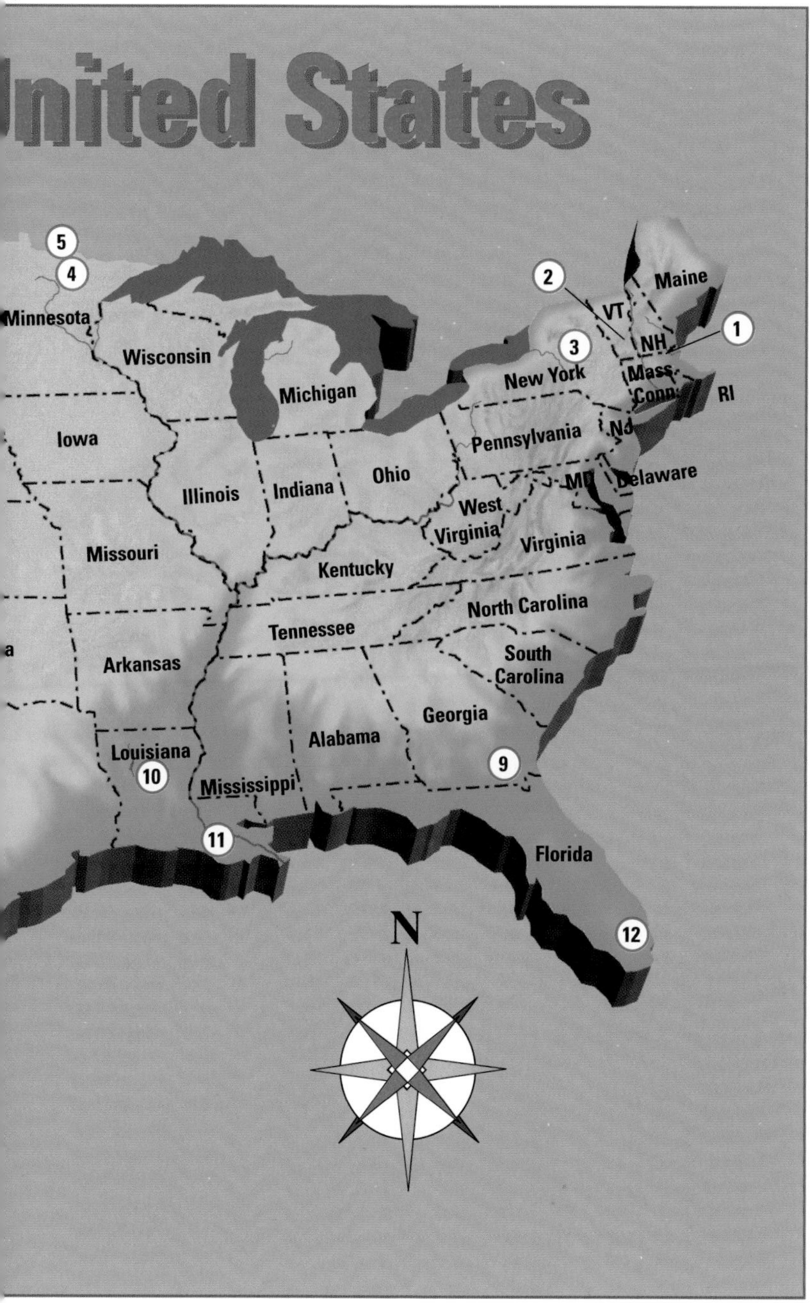
nited States
5
4
Minnesota
Wisconsin
Michigan
Iowa
Illinois
Indiana
Ohio
Missouri
Kentucky
Arkansas
Tennessee
Louisiana
10
Mississippi
11
Alabama
Georgia
9
Florida
12
2
3
New York
VT
NH
Maine
1
Mass.
Conn.
RI
NJ
Pennsylvania
MD
Delaware
West Virginia
Virginia
North Carolina
South Carolina
a
N

a Girl Scout adventure into Revolutionary War history around the Concord Bridge, and I recently revisited the peaceful national wildlife sanctuary on the Concord River that gets me away from metropolitan Boston traffic. I felt like I was miles from civilization. In the fall, the stunning reds and golds of maples on the riverbanks provide a pleasant canoeing experience, less hectic than "leaf-peeping" by automobile.

One of the best times to visit New York's 6-million-acre Adirondack Park is autumn, after the crowds vacate the expanse, lined with more than 120 miles (193 km) of designated paddling routes along quietly flowing rivers. My favorite trip is the Raquette River from Long Lake to Tupper Lake, where I'm sure to see fishers rowing vintage Adirondack guide boats.

The Raquette River in New York.

THE NORTHERN PLAINS

Near the U.S.-Canadian border in Minnesota and Wisconsin, thousands of glistening lakes and meandering rivers offer some of the best wilderness canoeing in the country. Minnesota alone has 3,000 miles of rivers (many of them flatwater streams) and 12,000 lakes. The Boundary Waters Canoe Area is the best known, but experiences like the smaller Voyageurs National Park to the west shouldn't be overlooked.

The U.S. National Forest Service and Minnesota's Department of Natural Resources have developed these densely forested areas for canoeing, with handy outfitting services at park entrances and camping sites at intervals for easy paddling days; the Boundary Waters area has 2,000 campsites. Your chances of seeing black bears are fairly high, as my friends learned at the end of a long day when they had to paddle past several sites that seemed to be the playground for a collection of bears.

Bear sightings motivate you to camp cleanly; you don't want bears to be attracted to your leftover food. Unfortunately, some have learned to associate humans with food, and I've packed up and left a camp to avoid a persistent bear.

Traveling in Minnesota you can experience the role of fur trapping in developing the continent's northwest. At Grand Portage National Monument, I stood at the old fort used for trading by the French and the Chippewa and watched a group of eight paddlers celebrate their completion of the grand portage. They had taken 3 weeks to travel from International Falls on the U.S.-Canada border along the Pigeon River; the trip finishes with an 8.5-mile (13.7-km) portage around crashing cascades to Lake Superior. Though perhaps not a good choice for a first long trip, the journey takes you over a rough trail that voyageurs traversed in 3 hours carrying up to 180 pounds of furs and goods.

THE WEST

This region is known largely for the spectacular whitewater rivers that tumble from high mountains. But the geologic grandeur of the West is accessible to beginning canoeists, who can travel deep into the canyons of the 117-mile lower Green River in Utah. Here is a perfect introduction to canoe camping, with miles of sites on sandy beaches set against sandstone cliffs and slick-rock waterfalls.

If you want an effortless trip, the Green River is a good float. Friends I've traveled with in the Canadian Arctic decided to canoe the Green over 10 days. They began paddling with the same vigor they use up north and ate up the miles so quickly they almost reduced the trip to a few days.

Texas's Rio Grande.

They slowed down and began to explore exquisite side canyons with sheltered pools perfect for swimming and striated rock formations that glow in the afternoon sun. If you want relaxation, take this trip.

Some of the best western canoeing (and fishing) happens on its back-country lakes, such as Yellowstone Lake in the first U.S. national park. The lake, like the west in general, is a huge, open expanse subject to unrestrained blasts of wind. Fortunately, Yellowstone Lake has numerous inlets for protection, but I recommend avoiding any long crossings on large western lakes.

I found better protection on the smaller lakes in Glacier National Park in Montana, although the long, narrow profiles of St. Mary and McDonald lakes tend to funnel the wind. St. Mary is one of the most photographed lakes for nature calendars, and I recognized the stark backdrop of the snow-topped mountains immediately. Go in early July, just after Going-to-the-Sun Road opens; the wildflowers crowding lowland meadows encourage endless photos. The park service makes trips easy with nearby canoe rentals.

THE SOUTH

The tangle of cypress forests and swamps in the south provides a maze of waterways to explore. One of the largest and best canoeing wetlands is the Okefenokee Swamp in Georgia, where a spring trip offers mild temperatures, high water, and blooming wildflowers. The Saline Bayou in the heart of Louisiana takes you into a dense pine-and-hardwood forest, while the Atchafalaya Basin mixes hardwood forest with swamp.

The Atchafalaya offers a great combination—crayfishing and canoeing. The locals can tell you how to catch crayfish with a net and bait and then how to boil them up into a tasty camp stew. Explore the secluded networks of bayous and small lakes away from bustling boat landings at the edge of the swamp. In the backwaters you'll find wildlife watching that rivals the Florida Everglades.

The Everglades region is well known for a reason. Its clear, shallow rivers make it a canoeist's paradise, with four canoe trails and a 99-mile wilderness waterway that you must share with motorboats. I'm not as avid a bird-watcher as my husband, but even I could find satisfaction here in observing the large, flamboyant birds that are amazingly calm about canoeists floating past. Birds congregate on sandbars and islands (the rangers can tell you which have restricted access), and children can do a "rainbow hunt" to identify reddish and snowy egrets, pink flamingos, white ibis, roseate spoonbills, Louisiana herons, and brown pelicans with wingspans longer than a tall adult. If you're lucky, you'll see iridescent purple gallinules walking on lily pads.

Winter and spring visits to Florida are best to avoid the rainy season and extreme heat, but be careful even then. A northern friend who said he never burns didn't believe what he was told about the intensity of the sun, and he neglected to bring sunblock. That night he was wrapping cold, wet towels on his fiercely sunburned legs after spending the day in the aluminum canoe that he'd rented. Cover up, bring plenty of sunblock, and avoid the reflective-oven effect of a shiny canoe.

Alligators are plentiful in the Everglades, but they leave you alone if you give them space. A friend who ran beginner canoe trips here for almost a decade never had a problem with them. Still, the sight of a gator as long as your canoe is pretty impressive!

ALASKA

Alaska's waters range from clear, spring-fed lakes and salmon-fishing streams to the opaque, milky-colored rivers flowing from glaciers. What doesn't change is the water temperature—cold, cold, cold, even in the middle of the very brief northern summer.

Alaska offers a wealth of backcountry paddling opportunities, and it's wise to hire local guides in remote northern sections like the Brooks Range. It usually means the additional expense of a float plane trip north from Fairbanks, but this is Alaska! You'll never regret it.

We discovered more accessible trips from the triangle of roads between Anchorage, Fairbanks, and Tok Junction when we logged almost 2,000 road miles (3,218 km) getting to various canoeing areas. Alaskans are used to driving long days to get anywhere, and after a while, we found ourselves agreeing that a 700-mile (1,126-km) journey was just fine to get to the next spot.

The Kenai National Wildlife Refuge offers a 60-mile (96-1/2-km) canoe loop on the Moose River, which links 30 lakes, but be ready to portage between some of the lakes. The 80-mile (129-km) Swanson canoe route is marshier, and campsites are harder to find, but the fishing makes up for the inconvenience. The current is slow, and sometimes low in late summer, but by then the worst of the insect season is over. Yes, the mosquitoes and black flies can be abundant. Because the best water is often found when the insects are thickest, I get used to applying repellent like cologne, and I become almost oblivious to the bugs. Really! You must register at one of the park entrances for a backcountry permit, because the Kenai canoeing takes you into the interior of the refuge—moose country!

The Nancy Ponds area provides a taste of Alaska's glacial history, where the lakes and meandering streams flow beside elongated glacial deposits called *drumlins*. These narrow, gentle mounds show you the direction in which the glacier travels, and I was captivated by their beauty against the snow-topped peaks of the surrounding Talkeetna and Chugach mountains. Canoe travel is a little more civilized here, particularly for families. You can rent cabins if you don't want to camp, and canoe rentals and shuttles can be arranged easily with local outfitters.

In Alaska, canoeing and fishing go together. My favorite canoe meal is fresh-caught salmon, because summertime paddling coincides with the famed salmon runs. The most impressive fishers are the bald eagles who work the river. I saw 14 on one memorable cruise (I lost track of the number of osprey), and my Alaskan friends assured me it was a slow day.

THE U.S. TRAVELOGUE

Permits

Access to most American flatwater rivers and lakes is still guaranteed through public access sites, and river travel is often possible without permits. However, individuals do need permits for some protected rivers like the Green in Utah. Groups must obtain permits to travel in national forests and parks and in some state preserves like New York's Adirondack Park. Always check the permit situation with local outfitters or regional government agencies.

Camping

Fees are often charged at easily accessible public campgrounds, whereas backcountry camping is often free but requires permits. In popular canoe camping areas like Minnesota's Boundary Waters, you must make reservations with park authorities to be allowed to camp and to be assured of a site.

Rules and Regulations

State regulations vary on the use of flotation devices. Some require only the presence of one flotation device per person in the boat; others require that canoeists wear the devices or wear them during specific seasons. Check the regulations with a local boat shop or state authorities.

For Information

To find regional and local information, contact the National Association of Canoeing Liveries and Outfitters, P.O. Box 248, Butler, KY 41006 (telephone 606-472-2205).

Canoe Canada

Many people dream of traveling Canada's wilderness waterways, which have lured outsiders since the canoe travel of the native Indians and Inuits captured their imaginations in the early 1800s. The only problem is deciding which beautiful region to explore in a nation that offers more than a million square miles of wilderness. Canada's lure is its vastness and the opportunity to truly cast off the restrictions of a civilized existence and travel for an extended period without seeing other humans.

I know Canada's north better than my own Canadian cousins do, because I've explored the tundra on wilderness trips into the Northwest Territories and northern Quebec for the last 12 years. (My relatives, who like to vacation in U.S. resorts, haven't been consumed by this fascination with their Arctic lands.) I help introduce beginners to wilderness canoe travel when I colead journeys called Arctic Barrens Expeditions. In a 2-week orientation period, we train people who have never paddled or camped before to handle the rigors of 2-month trips. Many find it the most rewarding experience of their life. I certainly do, which is why I keep returning.

You can embark on a peak wilderness experience of just a few days or many weeks. Independent travel is an option for the experienced canoeist, but Canada offers beginners a wealth of guided opportunities through its nationally funded tourism agencies and well-developed provincial canoeing associations. Take advantage of this expertise for your personal safety and enjoyment, particularly if your route is likely to introduce you to sections of whitewater.

THE ATLANTIC

Choose from protected Labrador fjords, with the world's highest sea cliffs, or the stark interior lakes of Newfoundland. Accessible by ferry, Newfoundland is an easier place to get a taste of raw tundra than the far-off north. Friends who have paddled in Gros Morne National Park rave about the unique perspective that you can get by hiking to the tops of these western fjords. They were particularly impressed by the boardwalks on the portages in the interior parks, because they're used to more primitive (muddy) conditions. The Canadians make travel easy in their canoe parks.

I first visited the Gaspe peninsula in Quebec to scope out the cross-country skiing, but I discovered the lake canoeing and fishing is accessible right off the Parc de la Gaspesie access roads. I have a weakness for French-speaking Quebec, largely because of the bakeries and pastry shops in the small villages, and my research guarantees that you'll find them

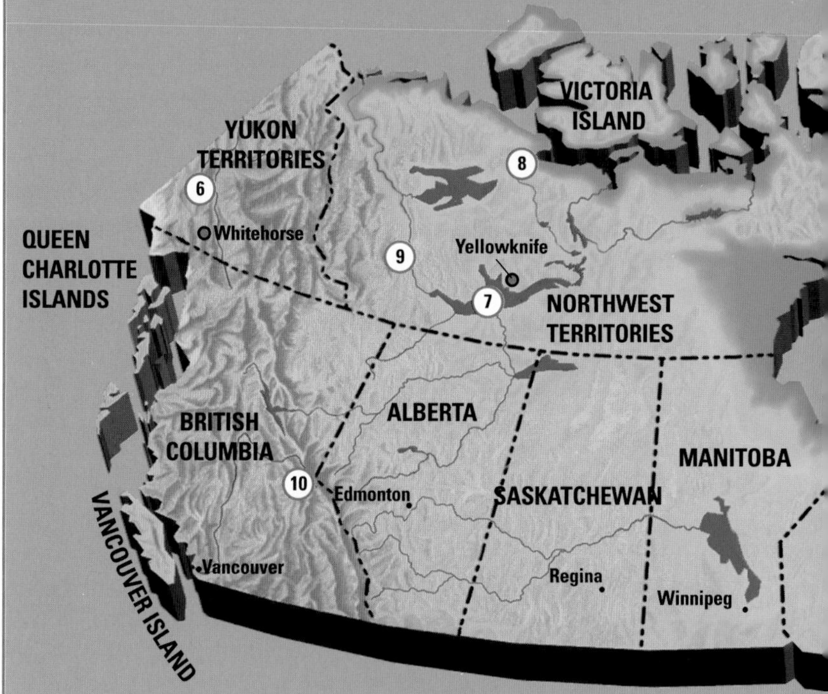

1 Bay of Islands, Nova Scotia
2 Algonquin Prov. Park, Ontario
3 Great Lakes
4 Quetico Prov. Park, Ontario
5 Parc De La Jacques Cartier, Quebec
6 Yukon River, Yukon Territories
7 Great Slave Lake, Northwest Territories
8 Coppermine River, Northwest Territories
9 Mackenzie and Nahanni Rivers, Northwest Territories
10 Bowron Prov. Park, British Columbia

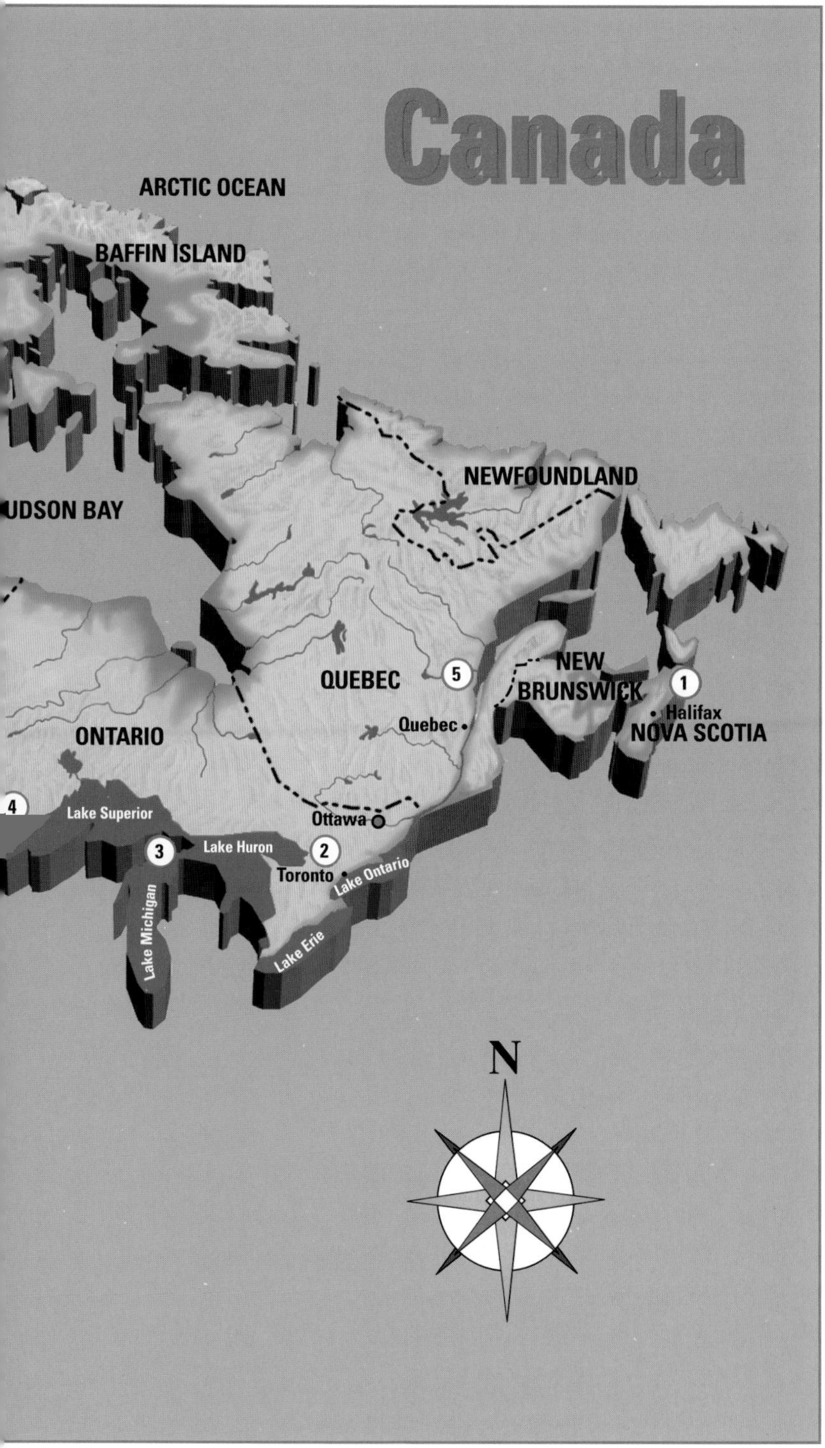
Canada
ARCTIC OCEAN
BAFFIN ISLAND
UDSON BAY
NEWFOUNDLAND
QUEBEC
5
Quebec
NEW
BRUNSWICK
1
Halifax
NOVA SCOTIA
ONTARIO
4
Lake Superior
Ottawa
3
Lake Huron
2
Toronto
Lake Ontario
Lake Michigan
Lake Erie
N

here. It's a great area for day trips, which begin with a stop at the local boulangerie for provisions, of course.

North of the St. Lawrence River, hydro-rich Quebec offers great canoeing in Parc de la Jacques Cartier, Parc des Grands-Jardins, and Parc du Saguenay. The first two parks are inland, but the Saguenay River is a deep, majestic fjord subject to tidal flow that empties into the lake. In July we saw a few whales and porpoises heading up the broad river (but the best time for whale-watching is August).

THE SOUTHERN SHIELD

Stark, rocky outcroppings have trapped thousands of lakes and streams that lured the fur-trapping voyageurs north into the boreal forests. Discover murals of Indian pictographs on ancient granite walls in this region north of the Great Lakes. The north shore of Lake Superior has a stark coastline, and canoeists should be very familiar with the topography before venturing out. Many beautiful bays with shallow beaches, like Pancake Bay, offer easy landings and great canoe camping, but other sections have steep cliffs with no respite from the wind. Treat this lake like the ocean—I've seen it look like the Atlantic. I've experienced a few crash landings, even on a sandy beach, and they take more skill than you may have at the beginning.

The lakes of Quetico Provincial Park in Ontario provide a less-traveled version of the Boundary Waters Canoe Area in Minnesota. The park is almost roadless, which guarantees a primitive experience. The quiet rivers allow easy travel and moderate portages, with options for short or long loops. Canoe rentals are easily accessible, and launch areas are plentiful.

Ontario's Algonquin Park is Canada's premier canoeing park, with 29 different access points for canoe trips and 1,500 kilometers (over 900 miles) of routes. Its array of services makes it a good destination for families. Kids can enjoy breaks from canoeing with nature hikes, museum visits, and evening programs. However, the park is incredibly popular in the summer, and even during my visit in late June, it was crowded. If you like people and want to meet other families, you'll find them here. Reservations for camping are essential.

NORTH OF 60°

Perhaps no area strikes the imagination more than Canada's north, where caribou in massive herds outnumber humans 20 to 1. A guided experience is highly recommended for these remote areas, particularly on the rivers, which usually involve some whitewater travel.

The gold rush country of the Yukon offers fast glacier-fed rivers, but its prime jewel of flatwater canoeing is Kluane National Park, a World Heritage Site. The longest glacial valleys in Canada can be seen from your canoe, and I spotted my first Dall sheep on steep hills surrounding the lake. Unpredictable high winds are a problem, so keeping close to shore is wise. The lake has an unusual blue-green color, which is spectacular on a sunny day. Canoe rentals are difficult to find, so bring your own.

The immense Northwest Territories range from the deep canyons and waterfalls of the Nahanni River (another World Heritage Site) to the rolling tundra of well-known rivers like the Coppermine, Thelon, and Back. The road ends in the capital, Yellowknife, from where canoeists experience the thrill of plane travel to northern headwaters. Go with a guide or outfitter, because most of these trips are an impressive mix of large lakes and whitewater rivers. More lodges dot the interior for fishing vacations, but an increasing number of natural history tours are available.

A side canyon in Kazan Falls.

THE WEST

Interconnected waterways in the Canadian Rockies link streams and alpine lakes into enjoyable canoeing circuits like the 117-kilometer (73-mile) Bowron Lakes Circuit in British Columbia. Older friends who prefer relaxed paddling have completed the Bowron loop with local guides, and the enjoyable trip gave them a remote experience without undue hardship. Paddlers can enjoy fishing and swimming on gentle rivers in all western plains provinces as well as the excitement of whitewater in the mountainous regions.

Although the Pacific coast lends itself more to sea kayaking (see p. 129 for a description of this paddle sport), ocean canoe tours on calm days let paddlers explore ancient aboriginal villages and sea-based wildlife in unusual places like the Queen Charlotte Islands north of Vancouver Island. One area on my list of places to explore is Barkley Sound on the west

Bow River in Banff National Park.

coast, which sea kayaking friends have recommended for ocean canoeing. The Broken Islands area in the sound provides a maze of islands for protection from wind, but it also presents an intriguing problem in navigation! Eagles are as common as gulls, and you can have fun searching for sea lions. Hire local guides if you are unfamiliar with ocean travel, because inclement weather can be a problem here. Rain gear is a must.

Waterways of Great Britain

The British quickly embraced canoeing when it was imported from North America in the mid 1800s, and in 1866 established The Canoe Club, the first such in the world. The almost 5,000 kilometers (almost 3,000 miles) of canals and navigable waterways in Great Britain still offer today's paddlers an unusual way to witness the history and culture of these islands. From your canoe you can find castles, manicured gardens, local pubs, and footpaths into the hills and dales, which invite hiking side trips. Many of the rivers are placid and friendly, and the lockkeepers are used to canoeists as well as the powerboaters with whom you'll share the locks.

ENGLAND

Exploring the Thames upstream of London offers a 240-kilometer (150-mile) trip that drops only 107 meters (350 ft) through numerous locks. The 64-kilometer (40-mile) stretch above Oxford features charming

THE CANADIAN TRAVELOGUE

Passports

Citizens of the U.S. without passports need two pieces of identification (a driver's license and a voter registration card, for example). All other visitors require passports, and in some cases visas.

Access

It may be necessary to get to some remote locations by rail or air. Canada has extensive air service by float plane in wilderness regions, with an infamous array of bush pilots ready to take you most anywhere. The southern provinces offer great canoeing accessible from public roads.

Emergencies

Anticipate that medical emergencies become more difficult to handle in remote regions. File your itinerary with a local outfitter (if you're renting canoes) or air carrier (if you're hiring transportation) and the Royal Mounted Canadian Police. A friend or relative should be aware of your trip's end date and be prepared to contact the proper authorities if you are delayed.

Weather

The country is so large that conditions vary greatly, but in general Canada experiences cool weather. Summer temperatures can range from 50 to 80 degrees F (10 to 27 degrees C) and cool greatly in poor weather. Northern areas feature long hours of daylight during the three paddling "seasons." Spring, summer, and autumn are compressed into a period between June and August in the far north. Anticipate that adverse conditions may delay your schedule, and figure "weather days" into your menu and itinerary planning.

Language

English is spoken in all provinces. French earns you a warm welcome in Quebec and the Maritime provinces.

For Information

Contact the Canadian Recreational Canoeing Association, 1029 Hyde Park Rd., Suite 5, Hyde Park, ON N0M 1Z0 (telephone/fax 519-473-2109).

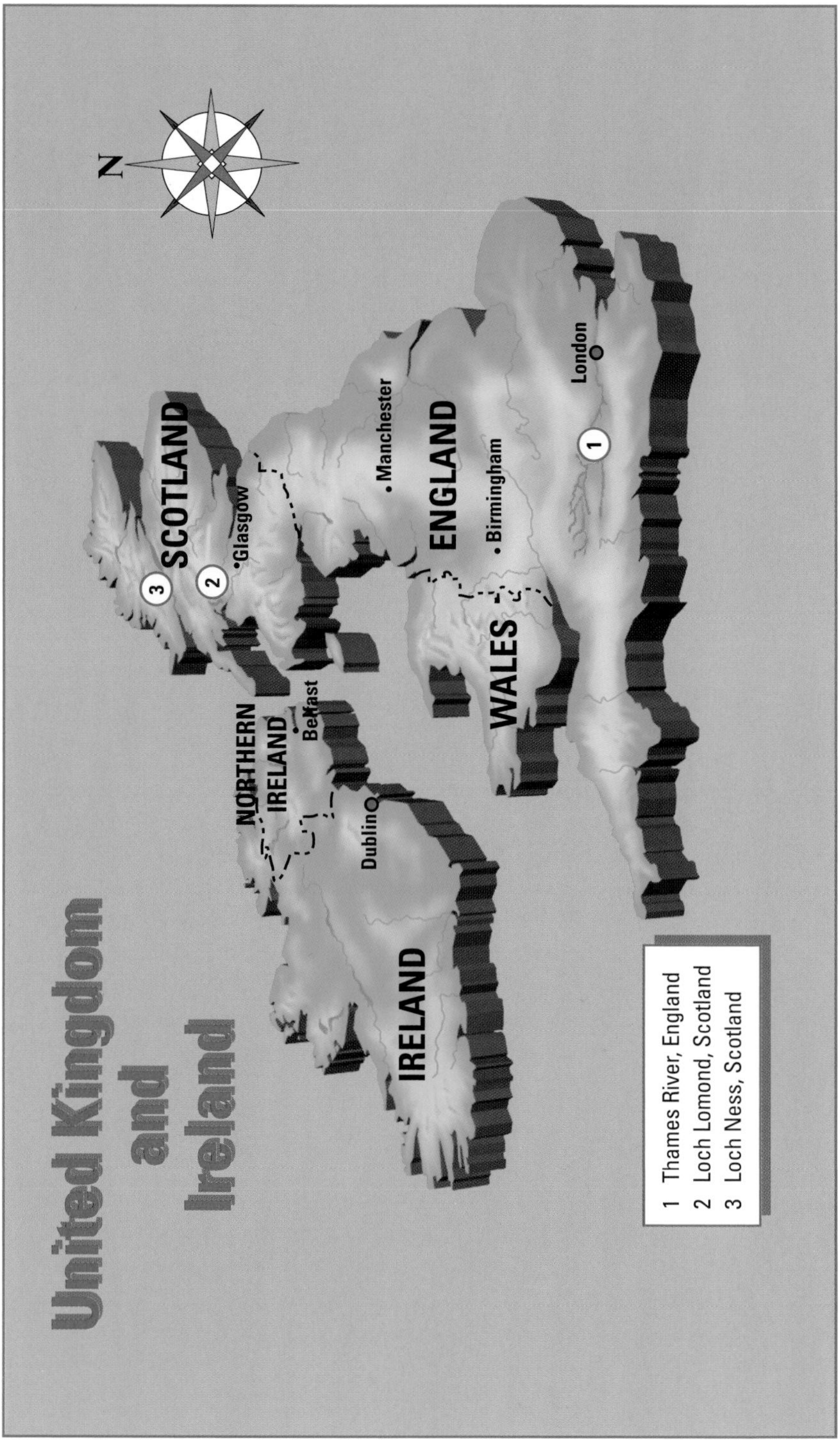
United Kingdom and Ireland
N
SCOTLAND
Glasgow
NORTHERN IRELAND
Belfast
Dublin
IRELAND
ENGLAND
Manchester
Birmingham
London
WALES
1
2
3
1 Thames River, England
2 Loch Lomond, Scotland
3 Loch Ness, Scotland

farms and pastures, while the next 97 kilometers (60 miles) downstream to Reading wind through the beautiful wooded hills between the Berkshire Downs and Chilterns. Visit Wordsworth's mountainous Lakes District in the northwest and the meandering rivers of the Norfolk Broads in the east, including a cruise past Cambridge University. Members of local canoe clubs can provide good insider's advice.

The Thames in Oxford. Photo by Phil Bibby/Outdoor Image.

SCOTLAND

The lochs (lakes) offer a real taste of Scotland's serenity and beauty as well as Celtic and clan history. The stark northern Highlands give a wilder feel; the mists of Loch Ness hang in one of the best-known areas to explore. Also explore the myriad islands in Loch Lomond, north of Glasgow. The Lothian region south of Edinburgh extending to the border features gentler wooded river valleys that wind through the moors.

THE BRITISH TRAVELOGUE

Private Waters

Many smaller rivers, including most of the fast-flowing rivers in England and Wales, are private, and canoeists cannot travel them as a matter of right. Consent to pass must be obtained from the owners of the riverbanks. Canoeists were rarely challenged on privately held lowland rivers in the past, but the situation is changing. Obtain approval, be courteous, and avoid the main game-fishing season in spring and early summer. This problem is not common in Scotland and Ireland.

Public Waters

Canoeists do have a legal right to navigate on nearly all tidal waters and on major rivers like the Thames, Medway, Wye, Severn, Stratford Avon, Trent, the Great Ouse, and Suffolk Stour, but access doesn't necessarily apply to the entire river. Check the situation with the authority for each river. A list of officers can be obtained from the British Canoe Union.

Permits

Traveling on public waters, including canals in England and Scotland, requires a license for which you pay a fee. Licenses for specific rivers can be obtained from the pertinent river authority. Members of the British Canoe Union can obtain licenses for some canals and "canalized" rivers as a benefit of their membership. Some canals also charge toll fees.

Weather

July and August are the warmest paddling months, with fewer crowds in September.

Camping

Permission must be sought from local landowners before you pitch a tent. It's best to make advance reservations at local campgrounds.

For Information

Contact the British Canoe Union, John Dudderidge House, Adbolton Lane, West Bridgford, Nottingham NG2 5AS (telephone 0602 821100). Request the *Inland Waterways Guide of Great Britain* from its book list.

Western Europe by Canoe

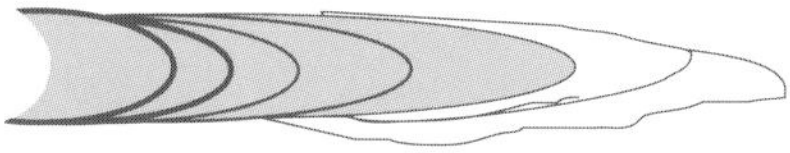

Try traveling in the wake of English barrister John MacGregor, who in 1866 explored more than 1,000 miles of European lakes and rivers and returned a year later to journey along the Baltic waterways of Scandinavia.

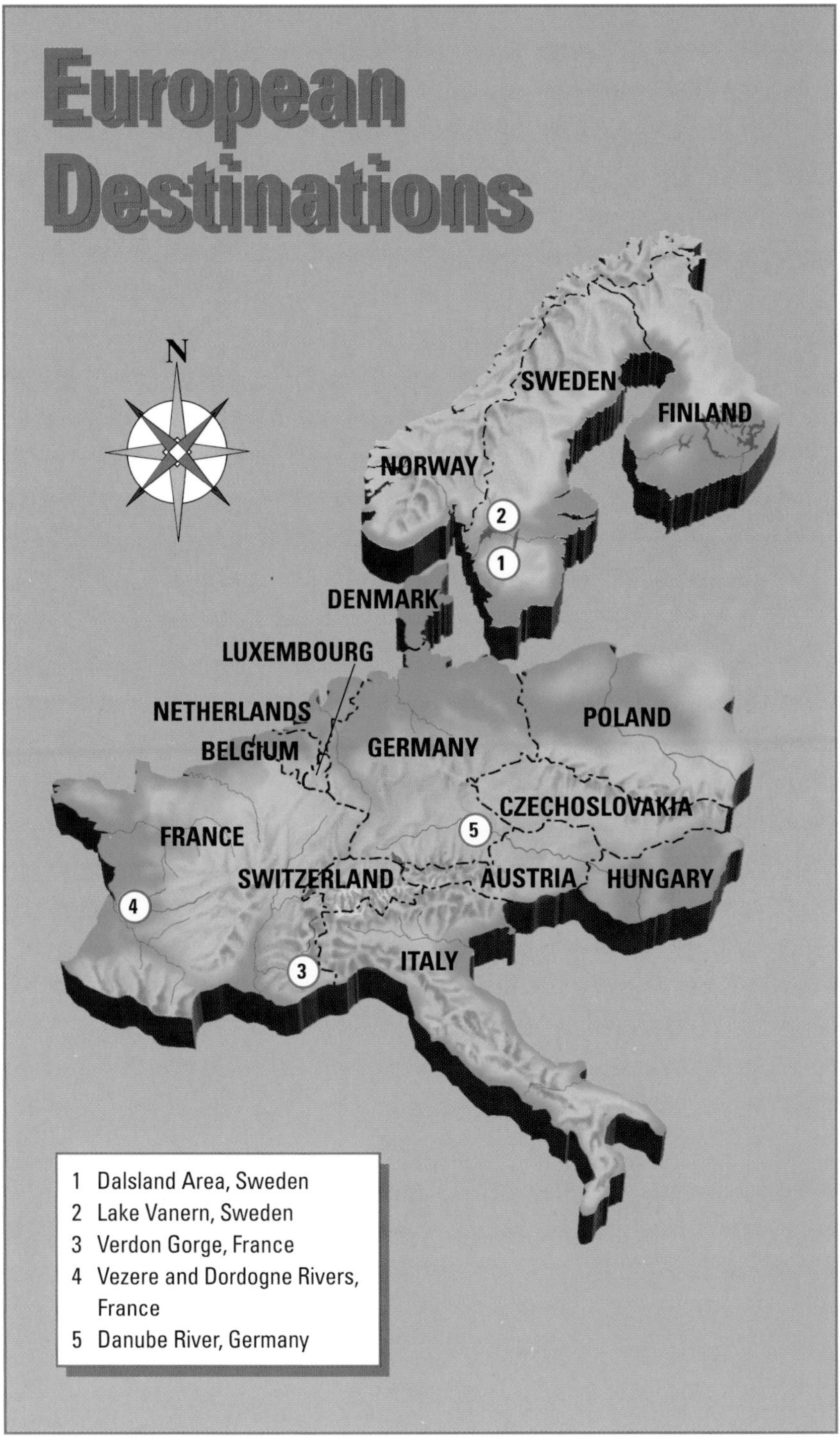
European Destinations
N
SWEDEN
FINLAND
NORWAY
DENMARK
LUXEMBOURG
NETHERLANDS
BELGIUM
GERMANY
POLAND
CZECHOSLOVAKIA
FRANCE
SWITZERLAND
AUSTRIA
HUNGARY
ITALY
1 Dalsland Area, Sweden
2 Lake Vanern, Sweden
3 Verdon Gorge, France
4 Vezere and Dordogne Rivers, France
5 Danube River, Germany

Keep away from the large, industrial rivers and you'll be able to discover modern-day versions of MacGregor's "charming voyages" abroad.

Western Europeans have an active canoe club system, with extensive facilities in riverside towns. Clubs organize trips, lessons, races, festivals, and clubhouse facilities, which often include accommodations for paddlers. Foreigners arriving by canoe can count on a warm welcome and generous hospitality from local paddlers.

GERMANY/AUSTRIA

The most picturesque cruise along the Danube River is a 530-kilometer (330-mile) stretch from Donauworth in Germany to Vienna in Austria. You pass 18 dams with a mixture of self-operated and large locks and a few civilized portages, all with well-graded trails and portage carts. Now this is portaging! Most major towns have canoe clubs with camping facilities.

FRANCE

Southern valleys like the Vezere and the lower Dordogne offer popular floats past ancient castles and prehistoric archaeological sites, with canoe liveries offering easy rentals. Visit Lac St. Croix below the Verdon Gorge. Easy access to vineyards and local delicacies makes canoe travel in France a gourmand's dream.

SWEDEN

The Dalsland Canal is a 272-kilometer (169-mile) network of forested lakes, rivers, and canals used solely by recreational canoeists and kayakers. Nearby is Lake Vanern, the largest in western Europe, with 22,000 islands. The canoe was imported late to Sweden (in 1935), but canoe liveries in the lake district provide full guiding and rental services.

FINLAND

Southern Finland is dotted with many nice lakes, while the north contains larger chains of lakes and rivers of varied difficulty. Lapland in the north features excellent lake paddling under a midnight sun, with a more temperate climate and prettier villages than northern Canada. Visit old gold rush sites on a river cruise through Lemmenjoki National Park.

THE EUROPEAN TRAVELOGUE

Passports

Americans need only passports, not visas, for European travel.

Permits

Individuals often don't need to obtain permits for canoe travel, but check with local authorities to be sure.

Temperature

Summer air temperatures reach 80 to 90 degrees F (27 to 32 degrees C), but water temperatures on dam-controlled rivers can be chilly. July and August have the fairest weather but the highest traffic. The canoeing season extends from May to September.

Camping

Tent camping is popular in Europe; campgrounds are easier to find near villages, but primitive camping is often the only choice. Obtain landowner permission.

Canoe Liveries

France has a highly developed national booking system through Office du Tourisme, 16 rue du President Wilson, 24000 Perigeux, France.

For Information

Contact the national governing body for canoeing in each country (see the appendix).

Scenic Australia and New Zealand

The world down under provides an unusual variety of paddling experiences—from urban tours in Sydney Harbour to the South Pacific ruggedness along the New Zealand islands. The best flatwater paddling in both countries is generally near the coastlines, where the rivers meander toward the sea. The famed outback, or interior, of Australia is largely a

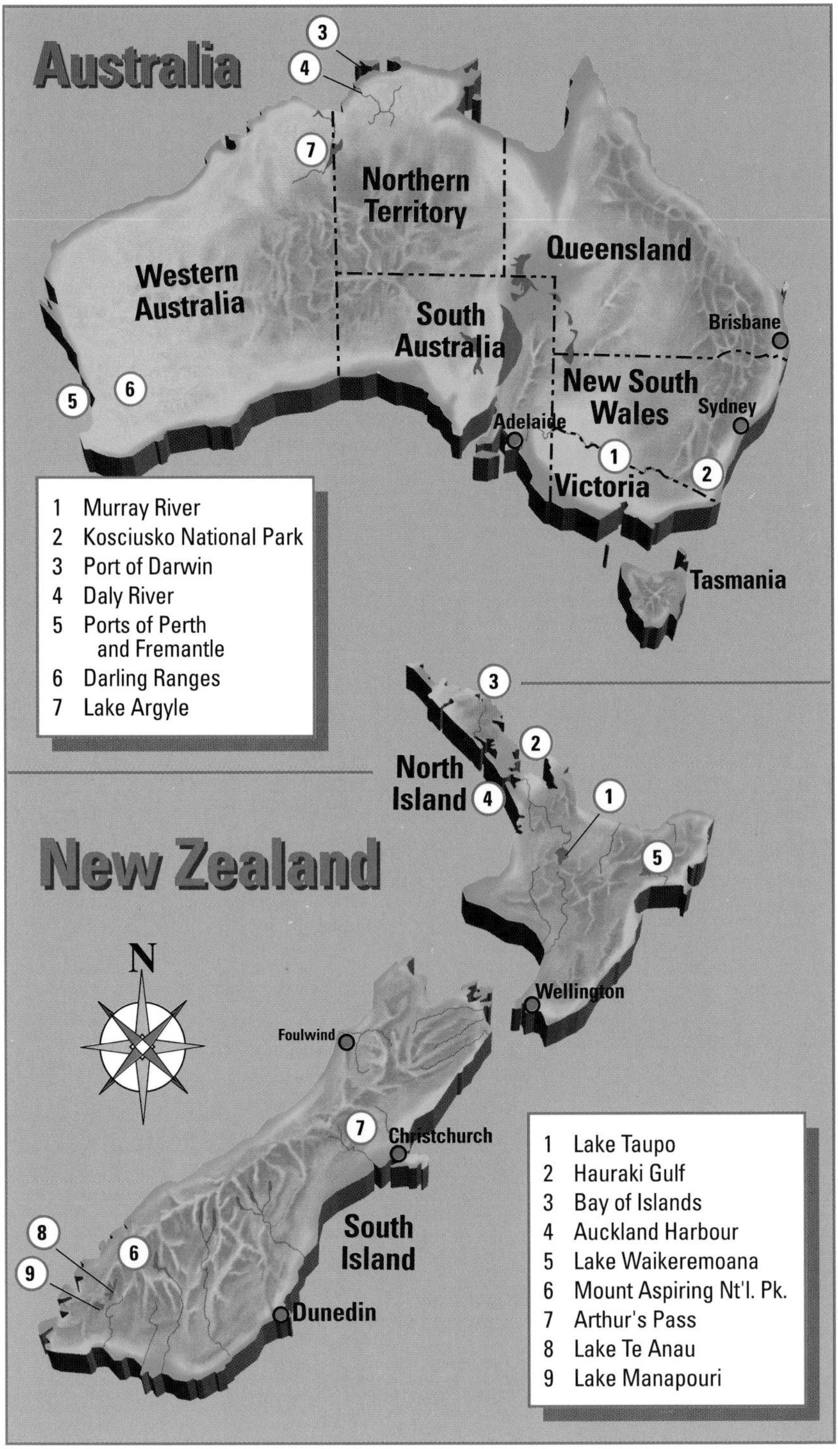
Australia
Northern Territory
Queensland
Western Australia
South Australia
Brisbane
New South Wales
Sydney
Adelaide
Victoria
Tasmania
1 Murray River
2 Kosciusko National Park
3 Port of Darwin
4 Daly River
5 Ports of Perth and Fremantle
6 Darling Ranges
7 Lake Argyle
North Island
New Zealand
N
Wellington
Foulwind
Christchurch
South Island
Dunedin
1 Lake Taupo
2 Hauraki Gulf
3 Bay of Islands
4 Auckland Harbour
5 Lake Waikeremoana
6 Mount Aspiring Nt'l. Pk.
7 Arthur's Pass
8 Lake Te Anau
9 Lake Manapouri

desert with few waterways to lure paddlers; New Zealand's interior is more famous for its steep whitewater rivers.

Getting here takes a long time—almost a full day or longer of air travel from most points. In Australia, you are wise to concentrate your travel in one region because the country is so large. For instance, the state of New South Wales ranges from a tropical climate in the north to the Australian Alps in the south, with 1,300 kilometers (808 miles) of coastline. Once you're in Australia, plan on staying awhile.

Because New Zealand is composed of two major islands, in-country travel can require additional time on ferries or by plane. The good news is that the ferry system is equipped to handle your boats as baggage.

Canoeing has a venerable history in the early settlement of New Zealand; Polynesians arrived by canoe and explored inland waterways principally by this mode of transportation. Many paddlers today associate New Zealand with challenging sea and river kayaking, but there's plenty of canoeing in a country with an estimated 2,000 navigable lakes, ranging from huge bodies like flooded Lake Taupo on North Island to smaller mountain tarns, or steep-sided lakes.

Australia

NEW SOUTH WALES

Sydney Harbour features three national parks with magnificent sandy beaches, stark headlands, small islands, rich fishing, and a lot of other boat traffic. Beware of swimming in calm water, where sharks can lurk. The Murray River rises in the mountains of New South Wales and empties 2,600 kilometers (1,600 miles) later into the sea in the state of South Australia. A fishing paradise, it also offers great bird-watching at many out-of-the-way spots along its length as well as plentiful canoe rentals. Boat launching facilities are available in most towns. Tributaries like the Murrumbidgee and the Snowy, with nearby Kosciusko National Park, offer canoeing experiences that range from lowland to alpine in nature. The 30,000 hectares (76,000 acres) of Myall Lakes National Park feature pleasant canoeing in eucalyptus forests and island camping.

NORTHERN TERRITORY

The Katharine Gorge region offers the best blend of inland Australia's calm-water rivers, gorges, and aboriginal mythology. Explore wildlife of the tropical coastline in the port of Darwin, and embark here for canoe tours and great fishing along the Daly River. Be aware that crocodiles may inhabit some coastal rivers, and they can be more aggressive than alligators.

WESTERN AUSTRALIA

The ports of Perth and Fremantle, home of the America's Cup, offer river and harbor cruising into wine and wildflower country. You'll find good canoeing in Walyunga National Park, where the Swan River pours through the Darling Ranges. The damming of the River Ord has created Lake Argyle, which rivals Sydney Harbour in size.

New Zealand

NORTH ISLAND

The Hauraki Gulf offers magnificent sea canoeing, and Auckland Harbour and Bay of Islands feature many protected tidal inlets. Lake Waikere-moana, rich in Maori history, has a vast array of coves and bays to explore. The best fishing is found here in the glacier-fed lake systems of Lakes Taupo, Tarawera, and Rotorua, the last of which also features thermal activity.

SOUTH ISLAND

Mt. Aspiring National Park with its 2,750-meter (9,000-foot) peak provides easy access for family canoeing. Also easily accessible are the river flats in Arthur's Pass National Park. Nelson Lakes National Park, a popular recreation area with great trout fishing, divides the rain forests of the west

Abel Tasman National Park in New Zealand's South Island. Photo by Glen Allison/ F-Stock.

from the dry grasslands to the east. While canoeing on Lake Te Anau, explore local caves and enjoy the glacier-carved mountains of Fjordland National Park. Nearby Lake Manapouri, one of New Zealand's most beautiful lakes, has been saved from hydropower development that would have raised the water by almost 12 meters (40 ft).

THE SOUTH PACIFIC TRAVELOGUE

Season

The summer paddling season runs from September to April (opposite to the northern hemisphere).

Climate

Australia is not considered a cold country. The hottest months are November to March. The rainiest months along the Great Barrier Reef are January and February. Spring high water in New Zealand is August to October. Expect rapid changes in wind, rainfall, and temperature there because of the island climate. River flows can change dramatically because of quick rainstorms. Local knowledge is essential.

Equipment

The cost of transporting your equipment and high import tariffs make local renting preferable. New Zealand manufactured equipment is available to buy or rent. Most imported equipment can be sold to avoid return shipping costs.

Access

Many popular touring rivers in New Zealand require access via private land. Obtain permission first, and realize that it may be denied during lambing season. The New Zealand Canoeing Association handbook (see the appendix) provides a list of property owners.

Ferry System

Boats can be transported as baggage in New Zealand for a small fee (about $15 U.S. each), but make reservations early—space is limited.

For Information

Contact the New Zealand Canoeing Association, P.O. Box 3768, 6000 Wellington (telephone 4-664772/732620) or the Australian Canoe Federation, P.O. Box 666, Glebe, NSW 2037 (telephone 61-2-552-4500).

Speaking the Language

A canoe isn't necessarily a canoe around the world! The traditional ''open canoe'' familiar to Americans and Canadians is called a canoe in North America, but the British call it a ''Canadian canoe'' or a ''Canadian.'' And what North Americans call a kayak is a ''canoe'' in Britain!

In countries like Germany and Austria, you may find signs along waterways that direct you to ''kanu'' clubs. Members of these local paddling clubs have a wealth of information and are delighted to help foreign paddlers explore their country—by canoe or kayak. The European club system for sport is the backbone of its paddling; most instruction happens through clubs, not at commercial paddling schools. The clubs have a long history of producing world-class paddlers, particularly kayakers who have trained on Europe's steep Alpine rivers.

Be specific when seeking camping accommodations in France. When the French say ''camping,'' they refer to developed campgrounds, sometimes with a bar and restaurant. ''Camping savage'' means an overnight in someone's field!

If you request information from the German Canoe Federation, ask for the English version of the information if you don't speak *Deutsch*. The federation produces a slick 544-page guide to *Deutsches Flusswanderbuch* with no translations into other languages, and the symbol system used to explain each river isn't enough to feel confident with the information.

Traveling by water gives me greater satisfaction than traveling by car or train, plus water travel better introduces me to new areas. Watery landscapes fascinate me, and I keep checking more rivers and lakes off my list of different regions and countries to visit. I once tried to explain to an Alaskan acquaintance why the landscape often appeals to me more than the intensity of the river. The thrills and chills of whitewater action motivated him to canoe, and by comparison my interest seemed tame. We weren't destined to be partners for long. It's important to follow your own desires and to enjoy where canoeing can take you.

6

PURSUING CANOEING FURTHER

Now that you have mastered the fundamentals of flatwater canoeing, you may want to expand your paddling skills and seek new challenges. Flatwater is excellent preparation not only for more advanced canoeing but also for other types of paddle activities. Think of them all as part of the same tree, with flatwater canoeing the main trunk of paddling experience. Whether you sit in a canoe or a kayak, many of the strokes and maneuvers are the same. You may easily transfer that knowledge and practice into other branches of paddling by making simple modifications to match the type of boat or paddle.

Your flatwater experience can also prepare you for more challenging paddling, such as whitewater canoeing or canoe racing. If you are intrigued by technical precision, then acrobatic freestyle canoeing can involve you in a choreographed canoe dance on water. And because your basic skills can also be easily adapted to river and sea kayaking, you can quickly become a versatile paddler.

Getting Serious About Canoeing

Evaluate your basic skills to determine whether you are ready for more advanced ones. If you can perform each of the important tasks I describe, then you are ready for more advanced paddling. If you cannot do some of the maneuvers, you need to practice them further with the help of a knowledgeable paddler or instructor. Then you'll experience greater success with a new canoeing endeavor.

Safety may also be an issue. If you plan to explore whitewater canoeing, then you need not only to be comfortable with the basic maneuvers but also to have good flatwater rescue skills.

ARE YOU READY?

If you answer yes to these important items, you are ready to explore other canoe sports.

1. I have acquired adequate conditioning to match the intensity of the new activity I want to try.
2. I have mastered these basic flatwater maneuvers:
   - Paddling straight
   - Spinning the canoe
   - Moving the canoe sideways
3. I have mastered these flatwater rescue techniques:
   - Self-rescue
   - Group rescue

Whitewater-Bound

Whitewater canoeing introduces you to an exciting new challenge. The river, now a moving playing field, demands that you act more decisively than on flatwater. You need the ability to quickly control your canoe on flatwater before attempting a whitewater river, where quick action is necessary to paddle successfully.

You are wise to get professional instruction for a successful introduction to whitewater canoeing. Experienced teachers can provide helpful feedback on your execution of maneuvers to make the transition less frustrating; they also provide invaluable rescue assistance should you tip over. Knowledgeable instructors will begin with calm-water practice of maneuvers and rescue skills before they guide you along progressively more difficult Class I-II rivers. (All rivers are rated on an international scale of river difficulty, from easy Class I to extremely difficult Class IV.) These rivers

Whitewater! Don't try this alone.

build from mild riffs and a few obstacles (Class I) to bigger waves and rocks that require increasingly quicker river reading and maneuvering (Class II).

Local clubs can provide not only basic instruction but also a calendar of river trips of varying difficulties. Paddling alone on whitewater is not recommended; clubs provide the support system necessary to paddling safely. Most clubs rate the difficulty of their trips and require that a canoeist have equivalent proficiency. Contact your national governing body (see the appendix) for a list of instructional schools and paddling clubs.

Freestyle Canoeing

The popularity of freestyle paddling has risen enormously in the last 5 years in the U.S., thanks to a devoted group of southerners who have promoted this intriguing variation on flatwater canoeing. Acrobatic in nature, freestyle canoeing lets you choreograph a series of intricate maneuvers that flow smoothly into a water dance. This activity is paddling's version of figure skating.

Dramatic boat leans combined with slow-motion maneuvers test your balance and precision, and the challenge is to stay upright as you create a dynamic visual image. Local and national competitions require that you perform various maneuvers set to music. Freestyle canoeing is perfect for those who have access to small ponds and lakes, and it challenges those who are intrigued by the precise execution of basic canoeing maneuvers. The American Canoe Association's freestyle committee is developing public programs and instructor certification standards.

For information, contact the ACA at 7432 Alban Station Blvd., Suite B-226, Springfield, VA 22150 (telephone 703-451-0141).

Freestyle paddling, an enjoyable water ballet, is catching on quickly in the United States.

Racing to the Olympics

Canoe racing is a venerable tradition thousands of years old for both inland and coastal cultures around the world. It has experienced renewed popularity in the last 25 years with the rise of "citizen's" races that attract hundreds of participants. The recent popularity of run-bike-canoe triathlons also draws beginning canoeists to recreational racing.

The serious canoeist has a number of opportunities to race in more organized competitions nationally and internationally. Local clubs and national organizations offer development programs to prepare young paddlers for these competitive disciplines.

Marathon

Usually longer than 5 miles (8 km), these races range as long as "ultra" distances of 250 miles (over 400 km). A common distance is 10 to 20 miles (16 to 32 km), which takes 2 to 3 hours. Racers use switch paddling to maintain both a straight course and speed. The U.S. Canoe Association recognizes a wealth of citizen's classes, including juniors, masters (40 years and older), families, aluminum, and plastic. As a result, marathon races represent a lively mix of opportunities that make it one of the largest and most competitive paddling sports.

For information on marathons in the U.S., contact the USCA, c/o Executive Director Jim Mack, 606 Ross St., Middletown, OH 45044 (telephone 513-422-3739). For information in other countries, contact the national governing body (see the appendix).

Marathon races are among the most popular and most competitive paddling activities.

Olympic Flatwater

Also known as sprint paddling, this sport has been an Olympic event since 1924. Canoeists in extremely tippy boats balance on one knee to paddle short distances in this high position. Distances range from 500 to 10,000 meters. The longer distances have been dropped from the Olympics but retained for World Championship events. In the U.S., the ACA's Sprint Committee and the U.S. Canoe and Kayak Team oversee this competitive discipline. For information, contact the USCKT, Pan American Plaza, Suite 470, 201 S. Capital Ave., Indianapolis, IN 46225 (telephone 317-237-5690).

Exploring Other Paddle Activities

Kayaking is an exciting activity that has grown dramatically in popularity in the U.S. in the last decade. My local paddling school now teaches many more lessons in kayaking than canoeing. A kayaker sits alone in a low boat, enclosed by a top deck except for an entry space, and uses a double-bladed paddle. The paddler gets great power from the two blades and can stroke strongly through pushy water. A stretchy spray "skirt" around the waist covers the entry to prevent water from flowing into the boat; this watertight system allows for easy paddling through waves.

The undersides of canoes and kayaks are not strikingly different when viewed from beneath the water. The boats turn in remarkably similar fashion, given the dynamics of water against any hull. A longer, narrower kayak tracks better and is harder to turn, just like a touring canoe. A shorter, wider kayak spins easily and is harder to paddle straight forward—just like a canoe with a similar design.

The transition from canoeing to kayaking is an easy one, because many of the flatwater strokes you have practiced can be used in a kayak. The major difference between canoeing and kayaking is rescue skills. Exiting a kayak is harder than exiting a canoe because you must remove the spray skirt to get out. Learning to exit smoothly and quickly is important practice at the beginning in flatwater before you paddle in bouncing water.

You are wise to seek instruction to experience a good introduction to kayaking. The feedback of an experienced instructor will help develop your paddling skills. Knowledge of ocean and river environments is essential to your understanding of their inherent hazards. Contact your national governing body (see the appendix) for a list of instructional schools and club programs.

Sea Kayaking

An explosion of interest in sea kayaking in the last decade makes these distinctive boats highly visible along ocean coastlines as well as inland waterways. The long, stable kayaks are relatively easy to handle, particularly with a rudder controlled by the feet. New kayakers find that they can move forward easily in a straight line with little frustration. The double-bladed paddle also provides amazing speed, which allows paddlers the reward of quickly exploring new places.

In addition to having paddling practice, you must know the marine environment to kayak safely. Before embarking on a sea kayaking tour you should know how to do these things:

Sea kayaking near Gulf Island in British Columbia.

- Read a nautical chart.
- Find your direction from charts and a compass.
- Navigate in traffic.
- Predict tidal currents and cross currents.
- Predict weather.

River Kayaking

The river environment offers kayakers different challenges—understanding the currents in the riverbed and negotiating around obstacles like ledges and rocks. The reward of river kayaking, like whitewater canoeing, is making quick and thrilling decisions as you find a route downriver. Stopping to play the river's currents can also provide dramatic enjoyment.

The best progression begins on calm water, where you refine your maneuvers as well as practice exiting the boat properly. Then select an appropriate river practice site with mild current, where you can learn to handle this added variable and develop quicker reflexes. Continue your practice in Class I-II river sections only after you feel confident in your ability to execute basic maneuvers and rescue yourself if you capsize.

Like the whitewater canoeist, a river kayaker needs to learn some essential points to paddle effectively:

- Turning into and out of eddies
- Ferrying across the river
- Reading river features
- Scouting and selecting a route
- Doing self-rescue
- Doing boat-assisted rescues
- Organizing a group on a river

River kayaking. For thrill-seekers only.

A Passion for Canoeing

I began my love affair with canoeing as a child in the backwoods in Maine. My father and his cousin had obtained an old cabin near Sebec Lake from Ted Whitten, a canoe builder in Dover-Foxcroft, who was no longer able to hike into the cabin. I remember peering over the edge of an unfinished wood-strip canoe in the shed behind his house, listening to this laconic man share his knowledge with us. I toed the shavings on the floor, smelling the wood and somehow sensing already that canoeing would become a consuming passion.

Ted had stashed several of his beautiful boats on the shores of small lakes beyond the cabin, for use in the days when he and his brother ran trap lines and fished the ponds. Too many people in the woods now, he would say, and we were among them, but I always believed he liked the idea of his canoes being used by people who appreciated their artistry.

To a 10-year-old, the 2-mile hike to the canoes seemed like a major expedition, but the trip was worth it—we were the only ones on these ponds, hidden in thick forest. I remember clear, cold water, 30-second swims, and a sense of well-being that I still seek when I canoe.

Since then, I've challenged myself with whitewater canoeing, dabbled with slalom racing, embraced marathon canoe racing for its fitness benefits, and explored sea kayaking to learn about a completely new environment. The possibilities have been endless, which I'm sure you'll discover.

I've taught hundreds of people to paddle and guided scores of canoeists in remote wilderness. My days in canoes are among the most memorable in my life, and I continue to find that feeling of well-being when I have a paddle in my hand. There are still many miles to paddle, many places to see. In fact, I think I'll paddle today.

APPENDIX
FOR MORE INFORMATION

Organizations

American Canoe Association
7432 Alban Station Blvd., Suite B-226
Springfield, VA 22150 USA
703-451-0141

The national governing body for canoeing in the United States, which develops instructional programs in six disciplines, promotes river conservation efforts, and supports the U.S. Canoe and Kayak Team in national and international competition; publishes *The American Canoeist* newsletter; offers a book service and film library.

American Whitewater Affiliation
P.O. Box 85
Phoenicia, NY 12464 USA
914-688-5569

A U.S. national organization that promotes recreational canoeing and oversees internationally recognized safety standards; develops river conservation projects; publishes a bimonthly journal.

Australian Canoe Federation
P.O. Box 666
Glebe NSW 2037
Australia
(2) 552-4500

The national governing body for Australian canoeing and kayaking.

Austrian Canoe Federation
(Osterreichischer Kanu Verband)
Berggasse, 16
1090 Wien
Austria
222-349203

The national governing body for Austrian canoeing and kayaking.

British Canoe Union
John Dudderidge House
Adbolton Lane, West Bridgford
Nottingham NG2 5AS
England
0602 821100

The national governing body for British canoeing and kayaking; publishes a list of water authorities for British rivers; publishes book list.

Canadian Recreational Canoeing Association
1029 Hyde Park Rd., Suite 5
Hyde Park, ON N0M 1Z0
Canada
519-473-2109

A Canadian national organization that promotes recreational canoeing in the 12 provinces; produces *Kanawa* magazine, devoted to Canadian paddling issues.

Federation Française de Canoe-Kayak
87, Quai de la Marne BP 58
94340 Joinville-le-Pont
France
1-45-110850

The national governing body for French canoeing and kayaking.

German Canoe Federation
(Deutscher Kanu Berband)
Berta Alle, 8 Postfach 100315
W-4100 Duisberg 1
Germany
203-721065

The national governing body for German canoeing and kayaking; publishes comprehensive handbook to German rivers.

Irish Canoe Union
House of Sport
Long Mile Road
Walkinstown Dublin 12
Ireland
(1) 501633 (x 2217)

The national governing body for Irish canoeing and kayaking.

National Association of Canoe Liveries and Outfitters
P.O. Box 248
Butler, KY 41006
606-472-2205

A U.S. organization of businesses that rent paddling equipment to the public. Some members also operate retail stores and schools.

Norwegian Canoe Federation
(Norges Padle Forbund)
Hauger Skolevei, 1
1351 Rud
Norway
2-874600

The national governing body for Norwegian canoeing and kayaking.

New Zealand Canoeing Association
P.O. Box 3768
6000 Wellington
New Zealand
4-664772/732620

The national governing body for New Zealand canoeing and kayaking; publishes a handbook that includes a list of property owners and addresses whitewater rivers.

Swedish Canoe Federation (Svenski Kanot Forrbundet)
Skeppsbron, 11
61135 Nykoping
Sweden
155-69508

The national governing body for Swedish canoeing and kayaking.

Switzerland Canoe Federation
(Schweizerischer Kanu Berband)
Obere Rebgasse 19
4314 Zeiningen
Switzerland
61-882000

The national governing body for Swiss canoeing and kayaking.

U.S. Canoe Association
c/o Executive Director Jim Mack
606 Ross St.
Middletown, OH 45044
513-442-3739

The governing body for recreational marathon canoe racing in the United States; conducts regional and national championships.

U.S. Canoe and Kayak Team
Pan American Plaza, Suite 470
201 S. Capital Ave.
Indianapolis, IN 46225
317-237-5690

The U.S. national governing body that oversees national and international competition in Olympic sprint canoeing and kayaking; oversees regional development programs for young racers; and designates Centers of Excellence clubs to promote the sport.

Publications

American Canoe Association Book Service
7432 Alban Station Blvd., Suite B-226
Springfield, VA 22150
703-451-0141

Ask for its catalog of paddling books and videos.

canoe
P.O. Box 3146
Kirkland, WA 98083
800-678-5432

Monthly magazine devoted to paddle sports; publishes annual buyer's guide.

Canoe and Kayak Racing News
P.O. Box 3146
Kirkland, WA 98083
800-692-2663

A tabloid newspaper with in-depth information about U.S. national and international competition as well as fitness for paddling sports.

Paddler
P.O. Box 775450
Steamboat Springs, CO 80477
303-879-1450

Monthly magazine devoted to paddle sports.

Videos

Cold, Wet and Alive by Nichols Productions for the American Canoe Association

An excellent educational tool for club and school programs to address the prevention of hypothermia in river situations or in outdoor settings in general. 23 minutes.

Path of the Paddle: Quietwater by Bill Mason

A beautifully filmed video by a respected and beloved Canadian paddler covering basic paddling strokes and maneuvers. 54 minutes.

River Runner Workout by Amy Schenck

A conditioning video with exercises and routines that simulate the muscular action in paddling. 40 minutes.

Solo Canoeing: Whitewater Bound by Tom Foster

A helpful video to guide flatwater practice of whitewater strokes and maneuvers, modeled in a useful progression for personal practice. 2 hours.

Song of the Paddle by Bill Mason

A memorable wilderness adventure for the family that explores the art and joy of canoe tripping with children rather than the technical elements. 40 minutes.

Special-Interest Books

Canoeing and Kayaking Instruction Manual by Laurie Gullion

The American Canoe Association's comprehensive reference manual for instructors teaching flatwater, moving water, and whitewater canoeing. Useful reference for students after initial instruction. 121 pages. 1987.

Canoeing and Kayaking for Persons with Physical Disabilities Instruction Manual by Anne Wortham Webre and Janet Zeller

An excellent American Canoe Association resource with practical expert advice on specific disabilities, effective teaching styles, and helpful equipment adaptations. 112 pages. 1990.

Canoe Racing by Peter Heed and Dick Mansfield

A useful training guide to marathon and downriver racing, with helpful advice on buying the right equipment, technique, training, and race strategies. 248 pages. 1992.

Canoe Tripping with Children by David and Judy Harrison

Tips on meal planning, equipment, first aid, and water travel, with activities geared to the abilities and short attention spans of children. 140 pages. 1990.

Freestyle Canoeing by Lou Glaros and Charlie Wilson

A technical guide to freestyle maneuvers that helps you understand the basic moves and combine them in water choreographies. In press.

CANOEING LINGO

amidships—The middle of the canoe.

backface—The side of the paddle blade that has no pressure against it during a forward stroke. Opposite side of the powerface.

beam—The widest part of a canoe; usually at or behind the middle point of the boat.

blade—The part of the canoe paddle that is placed in the water.

bow (rhymes with *cow*)—The front section of the canoe.

bow seat—The seat in the front of the boat; location allows room in front for the bow paddler.

catch—The beginning of a stroke.

centerline—A line (usually imaginary) along the canoe's bottom, running from bow to stern.

deckplates—Plates at the bow and stern that attach to the gunwales and deflect water.

depth—The distance between the gunwales and the bottom of the canoe, measured at the centerline at the boat's deepest point.

draft—The distance between the waterline and the bottom of the canoe; the degree to which a canoe rests below the water.

draw—Paddle stroke that moves the canoe strongly toward the paddle blade.

eddy resistance—The area behind a canoe's widest point where water and wind are displaced and create a swirl of unstable currents as the boat moves forward; weaker pressure occurs against the canoe.

exit—The end of a stroke, when the paddle is removed from the water.

feather—A recovery of the blade so that the paddle is above the water and flattened to the water surface to minimize wind resistance.

flare—Progressive widening of the hull from the waterline to the gunwales to deflect water and increase stability in rough water.

forward sweep—A paddling stroke that turns a canoe bow away from the paddle blade. The paddle is held parallel to the water during a sweep.

freeboard—The distance between the waterline and the gunwales; the degree to which a canoe sits above the water.

freestyle—A type of canoeing that involves acrobatic moves set to music.

frontal resistance—The force of wind and water against the leading end of a boat; frontal resistance exerts greater pressure against the boat than eddy resistance because it strikes the boat first.

grip—The top of a paddle shaft, where the canoeist grabs the paddle.

gunwales—The rails along the edges of the hull.

hull—The main body of a canoe stripped of any additional parts.

keel—A strip running the length of a canoe's underside that stiffens the hull and aids in tracking; a flatwater keel extends an inch or more into the water.

maneuver—The effect of a paddle stroke on a canoe.

offside—The direction of a maneuver in which the boat moves away from the bow canoeist's designated paddling side.

onside—The direction of a maneuver in which the boat moves toward the bow canoeist's designated paddling side.

painter lines—Lines attached to the bow (bow line) and stern (stern line) of a canoe.

pear grip—A paddle grip rounded like a pear that fits against the canoeist's palm and enhances power stroking.

personal flotation device (PFD)—A vest-style jacket filled with foam panels or tubes that provide buoyancy.

pry—Paddle stroke that moves the canoe strongly away from the paddle blade.

powerface—The side of the paddle blade pressed against the water during a forward stroke.

power phase—The part of a stroke when the body applies force against the blade; the blade is perpendicular to the water force for maximum power.

recovery—The part of a stroke when the blade is returned to the catch; it can be above the water (*feather*) or below (*slice*).

reverse sweep—A paddling stroke that pulls the canoe bow toward the paddle blade.

rocker—The degree to which a hull curves up at the ends; with increased rocker comes increased turning ability but decreased tracking ability.

shaft—The narrow neck on a paddle between the grip and the blade. A straight shaft has no angles from grip to blade; a bent shaft creates a 5- to 17-degree angle between blade and shaft.

shoe keel—A modified strip that runs the length of the canoe's underside; about a half inch deep, it allows more sideways maneuverability than a standard keel. Also called a shoeplate keel.

sideslip—A maneuver in which a canoe moves sideways and maintains the same alignment.

slice—A recovery of the paddle below the water surface to the catch; the blade is usually parallel to the oncoming water to minimize water resistance.

solo canoeing—Canoeing in which one person controls the boat.

spins—A maneuver in which the boat turns in tight circles.

stem—The part of the bow where the sides of the canoe meet; similar to the prow of a ship.

stern—The back section of a canoe.

stern seat—The seat closer to the end of the boat in a canoe.

strokes—What you do with a paddle that causes a canoe maneuver.

switch paddling—A style of canoeing that uses a cadence of forward strokes and a switch of paddling sides rather than corrective strokes to maintain a straight course.

tandem canoeing—Canoeing in which two people control the boat; the bow paddler controls the front and the stern paddler the back.

T grip—A paddle grip shaped like a *T* that offers precise control of the blade angle.

thwart—A crosspiece between gunwales that gives shape to the hull.

trim—Balance that puts a canoe level in the water; paddlers and gear can be shifted to achieve trim.

tumblehome—The inward curve of the hull from its widest point to the gunwales.

waterline—The highest point that water reaches on the hull when the canoe is in the water.

whitewater—Turbulent, aerated water.

yoke—A thwart shaped in a curve for portaging the canoe.

INDEX

ABOUT THE AUTHOR

Laurie Gullion is one of the most knowledgeable canoeing instructors in the country, having worked as a self-employed canoe tour guide since 1980. She leads canoe tours in New England and serves as co-leader for Arctic Barrens Expeditions—an organization that guides paddlers on whitewater canoeing journeys into the Northwest Territories of Canada. She is certified as an instructor trainer and as a whitewater canoeing instructor by the American Canoeing Association (ACA).

Laurie is an outdoor education specialist in the Outdoor Leadership Program at Greenfield Community College in Greenfield, Massachusetts. She has contributed articles to *canoe* and *Paddler* magazines and has written numerous books on the subjects of canoeing and skiing. She is the author of *Nordic Skiing: Steps to Success*, *Ski Games*, *The Cross-Country Primer*, and *Canoeing and Kayaking Instruction Manual*—the national text of the ACA for canoeing and kayaking certification programs. Laurie received her master's degree in sport management from the University of Massachusetts at Amherst, where she now lectures on writing in the sport management program.

In addition to teaching and writing about canoeing, Laurie is an accomplished canoe racer. She was the national champion in the women's tandem and mixed tandem classes of the ACA Whitewater Open Course Championships in 1986 and she finished in 2nd place in 1987. In her free time, Laurie enjoys wildflower photography, mountain biking, and fitness training.

Acknowledgments

I would like to thank Alan Fortune for meeting the enjoyable challenge of producing photographs that satisfied both of us, and especially for the photos taken from the ladder in the rowboat.

A special thanks to these obliging friends who modeled at unusual hours to catch the right light: Amy Butcher, Tom Foster, Bea von Hagke, and Sienna Loftus.

For help with photographs: Lou Glaros, ACA Freestyle Committee; Dave Harrison, *canoe*; Peter Heed, USCA.

For assistance with props: Rob Center, Mad River Canoe/Voyageur; Tom Foster, Outdoor Center of New England; Annie Scarborough, Dagger Canoe; Dick Weber and Stan Wass, We-no-nah Canoe; Wildcountry; and Gery & Al's Sporting Goods.

For reviewing and commenting on the manuscript: National Instruction Committee, American Canoe Association.

For sheer cheerfulness as well as good advice: Holly Gilly, developmental editor.

For unending good humor about another manuscript with annoying technical details: Bruce Lindwall.

Thank you!

Photo Credits

Principal photographer: Alan Fortune. Additional sources include the following:

Pages 2, 100, 101, 109: Laurie Gullion

16, 75, 78-85: Wilmer Zehr

110: © Anna Sullivan/Unicorn Stock Photos

126: © 1993 Tom Spitz

127, 129: Dave Harrison/*canoe* magazine